RELEASE YOUR INNER ROMAN

By the same author:

THE ROMAN GUIDE TO SLAVE MANAGEMENT

RELEASE YOUR INNER ROMAN

A TREATISE BY NOBLEMAN
MARCUS SIDONIUS FALX

JERRY TONER

The Overlook Press
New York, NY

12/16

This edition first published in hardcover in the United States in 2016 by
The Overlook Press, Peter Mayer Publishers, Inc.

141 Wooster Street
New York, NY 10012
www.overlookpress.com
For bulk and special sales please email sales@overlookny.com,
or write us at the above address.

Cataloging-in-Publication Data available from the Library of Congress

Manufactured in the United States of America

ISBN: 978-1-4683-1370-3

1 3 5 7 9 10 8 6 4 2

CONTENTS

AUTHOR'S NOTE

I AM A ROMAN. I am one of that heroic people who have conquered the known world. I am also a highly successful Roman. My ancestors won glory on the battlefield, a tradition I have maintained with my distinguished service in the legions. I count the emperor as a personal friend, have recently been awarded a consulship and own estates worth many millions of sesterces. I have applied the same rigorous approach to all areas of my life – from making money, to acquiring a wife, to getting the gods on my side. No one is better placed to tell you the secrets of how to succeed the Roman way. Up to now you barbarians have had to settle for marvelling at the achievements of us Romans. But even barbarians can improve themselves. This guide will tell you all you need to know to bring out your Roman side.

There can be few men more in need of this book than Jerry Toner. He has the audacity to teach others about the great achievements of Rome when he has learned nothing from them himself. He studies 'ordinary' Romans when he could learn everything he needs from Rome's great heroes. His household is a shambles. His children run amok and treat him like some kind of domestic slave. He even lets his otherwise delectable wife dictate to him on matters on which any respectable woman should be silent. I have reluctantly to admit that he is living proof of the limits of self-help because, put simply, he has no inner Roman to release. But his shameful example need not hold others back and if his work enables my message to reach a wider barbarian audience then he will finally have achieved something worthwhile.

Marcus Sidonius Falx
Rome, Kalendis Ianuariis

COMMENTATOR'S NOTE

IT HAS ONCE AGAIN BEEN my dubious pleasure to work with Marcus Sidonius Falx. He is a larger-than-life character who has not a single doubt about the truth of his beliefs. In his eyes, the Romans were quite simply the greatest, most successful people ever to inhabit the earth. While there will always be some academic disagreement about how representative his opinions are of all Romans, there can be no doubt that his views give us an insight into the characteristics which many at the top of Roman society thought made it great.

Roman society did not believe in equality. What mattered was status. Whether it was conquering foreigners, punishing slaves or standing as patriarch over their families, the Romans were extremely comfortable with the idea of hierarchy. They did all they could to improve their position in society. This puts Marcus in the ideal position to instruct us on how to succeed in the modern rat race. The Romans also had no problem about showing off their wealth and power. Success and display went hand in hand. From giving great games to owning large numbers of slaves and feasting at banquets, the Romans treated such expenditure as a simple index of their achievements in life. There is no one better than Marcus to let you into the secrets of living the good life. The Romans also had clear targets that they went about achieving in an often brutally efficient way. This no-nonsense approach to getting what they wanted was applied to all parts of human existence, from romance to finance. There is much that is still relevant to today.

Marcus is a man of empire. I cannot be certain exactly as to his dates but his views seem to reflect the kind of outlook associated with the early empire of the first and second centuries AD. Needless to say, the opinions expressed in the following pages are not my own and it is not without some hesitation that I make them known to a wider non-Roman audience. But I hope that in doing so Falx's text will show that the Romans could behave in a remarkably similar way to people today, even if they valued a very different set of personal traits than those found in modern self-help books. The Romans inhabited a tough world where life was short and cheap. Most of them could not afford the luxury of individualism or personal development. I will leave it up to you to decide whether you wish to adopt these characteristics in your own life. A brief commentary at the end of each chapter puts Falx's words in context and also tries to undercut some of his more exaggerated posturing and appalling self-justifications. Used alongside the further reading at the end of the book, this will point those who want to find out more towards the underlying primary sources and modern scholarly discussion.

Jerry Toner
Cambridge, October 2016

CHAPTER I

THE HABITS OF HIGHLY
HEROIC ROMANS

M ANY DECADES AGO, the Roman people threw off the yoke of monarchy and exiled their arrogant king, Tarquin the Proud. In response, the Etruscan king, Lars Porsena, besieged the city of Rome in an attempt to reinstate Tarquin and squash the infant republic. It took acts of the greatest heroism ever witnessed to convince the invader that he could never win. You can have no better examples of the characteristics that have made the Romans the most successful people the world has ever seen.

The first concerns a young Roman of noble birth, Gaius Mucius. The ongoing blockade meant that food became scarce and the price of what little there was went sky-high. Mucius thought it was outrageous that Rome, having finally rid itself of its hated king, was now being besieged by the Etruscans whom they had often defeated in battle. He resolved to avenge this insult by carrying out a feat of great bravery. He decided to penetrate the enemy camp on his own and try to assassinate the foreign king. But after he had thought it over, he was worried that if he went without being specifically ordered to do so by the consuls, he might be spotted by the Roman guards and arrested as a deserter trying to flee the city in her hour of need.

So he went to the senate. 'Senators,' he cried, 'I am determined to swim across the river Tiber and enter the enemy's camp to carry out a glorious deed.' The senate could not but approve of so valiant a wish. Concealing a sword in his robe, Gaius therefore set out. When he reached the enemy camp, it happened to be payday and the soldiers were crowded round the royal tent where the money was being distributed. Gaius went and stood in the thickest part of this crowd. There he saw two men sitting on the royal platform. The problem was that they were both dressed almost identically and even looked similar. One was obviously the king but the other must have been an attendant. Gaius could not ask someone which was which, of course, because then he would have given the game away so he left it to luck to decide. He ran up to the two men and struck the nearest one dead. He tried to attack the other but was immediately jumped upon and seized. Sadly, fortune was not inclined to help on this occasion and it became clear that he had merely killed one of the king's attendants and not the king himself. Now he was hauled up before him.

Even here, in the highest danger, Gaius's great spirit was such that he was able to inspire more fear than he felt. 'I am a citizen of Rome,' he said firmly. 'I am called Gaius Mucius and I treat death with the same disdain, whether I am killing the enemy or he is killing me.

Bravery is part of Roman nature, as is suffering in silence, and I am not a lone wolf. Behind me stretches a never-ending line of men with the same passion for glory. So you, King Porsena, must decide. Do you want to carry on a war where you will have to fight for your life every hour of every day? Where you will find a hidden enemy constantly lined up to attack you? This is the war we Romans will wage against you!'

The king turned puce in anger. But he was also terrified at the thought of this kind of clandestine warfare being waged against him personally and threatened to burn Mucius alive if he did not tell him the details of what Rome was planning against him. Mucius laughed grimly. 'Look and learn at how we Romans will do anything in the hunt for glory,' then he plunged his right hand into a fire burning in a brazier on the side. With no motion, not a sound, or even a bead of sweat, Mucius stood while his hand was roasted in the flames. The king leapt up in astonishment and ordered the guards to pull Mucius away from the fire. 'You have hurt yourself more than you have me,' he said. But he was impressed. 'If you were one of my soldiers I would praise you to the skies,' he said, 'but, as a prisoner, all I can do is honour you by allowing you to go back to Rome.' Then Mucius reciprocated this generous treatment: 'You honour courage. So let me tell you openly what no torture could ever have extracted from me. Three hundred Romans, the flower of our youth, have sworn to attack you in this way. The task fell to me first but each will come in turn until fortune finally gives us the opportunity we need to kill you.'

The king was so unnerved by the prospect of facing hundreds of assassination attempts that he sent envoys with peace proposals to the Romans. Mucius himself returned to Rome, where the senate rewarded him with some land west of the Tiber, which came to be known as the Mucian meadows. The people of Rome gave him the nickname 'Lefty' to mark the loss of his right hand.

The second hero to show you what it takes to be a true Roman is Horatius Cocles. In the same way that Mucius thought nothing of burning off his hand to prove his toughness, many other Romans have voluntarily engaged in single combat in order to decide a battle, even though this has sometimes meant certain death. These heroes have thought nothing of sacrificing their own lives to save those of their fellow Romans or to save the republic.

During Porsena's siege of Rome, Horatius Cocles was engaged in combat with two of the enemy at the far end of the simple bridge over the Tiber that sat in front of the town. Suddenly he saw large enemy reinforcements moving forward towards him. Fearing they would be able to force their way over the bridge and enter the city itself, Cocles turned and called to the Roman troops behind him to get off the bridge as fast as they could and cut the ropes which supported it. While they carried out his order, Cocles stood at the entrance to the bridge and single-handedly kept the enemy at bay even though he was wounded many times. The enemy themselves were astonished at his strength, endurance and courage. Once the ropes were cut and the bridge had fallen into the river, Cocles hurled himself into the river even though he was wearing his full armour, deliberately drowning himself rather than be taken alive. He had no regard for his own safety, solely for his country and for the glory that future generations would attach to his name.

If there is one thing that has made Rome great, it is this: that young Roman men are inspired to emulate the noble deeds of their ancestors such as Mucius and Cocles. What lessons can you who live in softer, more luxurious times learn from these models of great Romanness? What principles can you apply to your own lives to make you more like them? This is not the kind of information you can find taught in schools. But you can find it in this book.

Can you ever hope to live up to the example of Mucius? The answer is an emphatic yes. To be sure, you may not be able to prove your mettle in so flaming a fashion. But does that mean you are destined to be subservient and a failure? The answer is an emphatic no. Fortune may have condemned you to live in an age of rust and iron, when men have no chests, but that does not mean you have no opportunities to display your inner steel. Does your barbarian blood also condemn you to ignominy? All men are descended from distant ancestors who have had some impact on their behaviour, to a greater or lesser extent. You cannot escape your family. But the true glory of a man is his character. It exercises a power greater than wealth and secures honour and fame. The Romans worked hard to inculcate and develop these personal virtues. It is this habit of glory that I believe I can teach even the lowest slave.

And, in truth, there have been countless examples of

men of the lowest rank who have raised themselves up in life. A former slave of mine started out in one of the chain gangs on one of my estates in central Italy. I quickly spotted his capacity for hard work and his eagerness to please and promoted him to the position of overseer. After many years of loyal service I finally rewarded him with his freedom and some land. Now this lowly man – his friends call him 'the farmer' – is master of his own modest household and possesses several slaves of his own.

Even emperors can be made outside Rome. Did not the deified Trajan himself, one of the wisest and most glorious emperors, whose army crushed the Dacians and who campaigned as far as the Euphrates in the East, whose booty paid for the great forum bearing his name, and to whom the senate gave the title of 'Best Emperor' – did he not come from Spain?

What is the secret to such success? In a word, it is piety. Those who acquire it and display it in all aspects of their life find themselves swept on to ever-higher achievements. Indeed, I have never known anyone who can be described as truly pious who did not achieve noteworthy success. On the other hand, I have never known any individual to distinguish himself, or to accumulate any reasonable level of personal wealth, who did not display piety. From these two facts I have drawn the following conclusion: that piety is more important for self-development than anything else, and certainly more important than what one learns in the usual forms of education.

What is piety? In short, it is the inner force that compels us to do our duty to our parents, to our country and to our gods. Its roots lie in the total authority that a father rightly holds over his children. Romulus granted this power, which was valid until the father's death. It gave him the power to imprison his son, beat him or chain him as he saw fit. If the father thought his son should work on a farm, then so be it; if he felt his daughter should marry, then she did as she was told. Back in those days, the father could kill his children or even sell them into slavery. All successful men owe their achievements ultimately to their fathers.

If my character has only a few blemishes, if few can accuse me of being greedy, mean or debauched, then it is all thanks to my father. He loved the land and thought little of anything you could learn at school. Instead, he whisked me off to Rome to be taught the skills a noble's son would need. If you had seen me then you would have thought me a raffish fop: dressed in the finest woollen toga, he spared no expense in showing me how to behave properly. I would be mad to be ashamed of a father like him. I certainly won't defend myself, like many do, by trying to blame all my weaknesses on him. In fact, I say the opposite. If I had the chance to go back in time and hand-pick my own parents then I'd still be happy with the ones I had.

Being a father is not easy. Sometimes the state must come first. Some Roman fathers when in office have, contrary to every natural feeling and impulse, executed their own sons because they placed a higher value on the interests of their country than on the ties of nature that bound them to their offspring. The great Lucius Junius Brutus, for example, who first founded our great republic when he led the uprising to drive out Tarquin the Proud and was elected one of the first consuls, found himself in the position of having to oversee the punishment of a group of conspirators who were attempting to reinstate the exiled king, a group containing his two sons Titus and Tiberius. This group of rich young nobles had been able to do whatever they wanted under the monarchy because they had been in the king's favour and could rely on his personal influence to help them. But now that they were all equal before the law they found their behaviour constrained and they complained that it had turned them into slaves. Kings could hand out patronage, but the law was deaf to flattery. They had therefore connived with the former king to bring about his return but the group's plot was betrayed. They were sentenced to be flogged and then executed. So inexorable was the law that it required the holder of the consular office to impose the punishment. He who should never have witnessed such a thing was destined to be the one to see it duly carried out.

The young nobles were all tied to posts. But none was watching them: all eyes were turned to the consul's children and to the consul himself. The consuls took their seats, the lictors were told to inflict the penalty. They beat the young men's bare backs with rods and then they beheaded them. During the whole exercise, the father's face showed how he was really feeling, with grimaces and cries escaping from his lips. But the father's stern resolution was even clearer. He was determined to do his duty and oversee the execution.

That is the kind of determination that won Rome an

empire. It is the mark of a good leader to put the interests of the mission first. To be sure, the unwavering courage of a Cocles is a benefit as is the self-control of a Mucius. Fortune is usually on the side of the brave in the same way that the winds and the waves help the skilful sailor. But it is the decisiveness and sense of responsibility that makes a true leader. This will make men follow you into an inferno if you so command them. As the elder Scipio said, when somebody asked why he was confident that his troops could defeat Carthage on their own on North African soil: 'There is not one of my men who would not jump from a high tower into the sea if I ordered him to.'

There are many causes of failure. Some are born into bad families and cannot escape from their influence. Others are born into good families but suffer a bad upbringing. Some lack purpose or ambition. Others procrastinate through fear. Some make bad choices in their wives. Others lack a suitable patron to help them on their way. But perhaps the greatest cause of failure is to lack the ability to get other people to do things willingly for you. Many try to force others to carry out their commands through fear. But, as the saying goes, a drop of honey catches more flies than a gallon of gall. Encouragement and respect gained through example will make people do what would otherwise never be in their own interest.

So far I have spoken only of men. But barbarian women also have much to learn from their Roman counterparts. Naturally, it is the case that women have a far narrower range of virtues than men. It is difficult for women to win praise in new areas of endeavour because their lives have less diversity in terms of opportunities. Their skills are defined by the unchanging requirements demanded by the home. For that reason, praise for a good woman is both simple and formulaic: her goodness does not need a variety or novelty of words to express it. Rather it is sufficient, when women have performed the same few deeds well, to praise them as a group. But despite that, some women do stand out as deserving individual praise, none more so than my mother. In modesty, moral integrity, chastity, obedience, wool-making, diligence and loyalty she is the equal to all other excellent women nor does she come second in terms of virtue or wisdom. She was faithful to her husbands and fair to her children (I was her child by a second marriage to a father now long since dead).

That war against Porsena, which has already furnished us with two fine examples of Roman heroes, can also provide us with a shining beacon of female behaviour. Indeed, it was the example of Mucius that inspired some women to seek public honour. As part of the agreement that ended the war between Rome and Porsena, a group of Roman hostages, both girls and boys, were handed over to ensure that the terms of the treaty were kept. One of the hostages was a young woman named Cloelia. But she fled the enemy camp, taking with her a band of other female hostages. First she made her escape by horse, then by swimming across the Tiber amid a hail of enemy spears. Not one of the girls was injured and Cloelia returned them all to their families. Once her escape had been noticed, Porsena demanded her return alone of all the escapees, a demand to which the Romans agreed. Once she had been returned, though, Porsena was, as he had been with Mucius, so impressed by her bravery that he allowed her to select half of the remaining hostages and for them to be freed and returned alongside her to Rome. Ignoring the Roman girls, she chose only the Roman boys so that they would be able to continue the war. Her singular devotion to duty meant that the Romans gave Cloelia an honour usually reserved for men: they erected a statue of her riding a horse, which was placed at the top of the Sacred Way.

If you, whether man or woman, are to aspire to these great heights, then you must, as the Delphic Oracle said, know yourself. Know your weaknesses and where you need to improve. Set yourself targets and push yourself to achieve them. Do you wish to be a praetor or a consul? Do you want to own many slaves? Do you desire a virtuous wife? All these things this book will help you do.

But such an increase in self-awareness and performance comes at a cost. The secret to Roman success cannot be obtained without paying a price, although the price is far less than its value. It will take hard work. The longer I live the more I am certain that the great difference between the weak and the powerful is energy, an invincible determination to win glory whatever the personal consequences. Not even emperors can escape the necessity for hard work. When Hadrian said to a woman who was hassling him for a hearing that he did not have the time, she replied simply, 'Then don't be emperor.' Study it carefully and you will find that this book provides you with all you need to Romanise all areas of your life. I have asked hundreds of the richest and most powerful Romans of my acquaintance for their opinions on what brings success. You too will be able to think like one of them.

Like Mucius, you must leave yourself no possible way of retreat. You must commit yourself totally and show no weakness. Only those who become glory-conscious ever accumulate it: your mind must become so thoroughly saturated with the desire for glory that you are already able to imagine yourself having it. You must be as hard on yourself as you would be on your enemies. When the great Julius Caesar besieged the last remnants of the Gauls in the town of Uxellodunum, he was determined to ensure that there would be no further rebellions in the province after his period as governor had ended. Having positioned his forces around the walls, he launched a diversionary attack up a ramp built specially for the purpose. He then ordered his troops surrounding the city to take up a war cry, thereby fooling the Gauls into believing he was about to launch a direct assault on the walls. Unknown to them, however, the Roman sappers had tunnelled to the spring that supplied the Gauls with water and used the diversion to finish the job of cutting the Gauls off from water. Realising the hopelessness of their situation the Gauls soon surrendered. Caesar accepted the Gallic surrender. He decided against executing or selling the survivors into slavery, as is usual. Instead, he had the right hands of all the surviving men of military age cut off so they could never again raise a weapon against their Roman masters. He also dispersed this mutilated mass of men throughout the province for all Gauls to see the futility of taking up arms against Rome.

All great men need to take tough decisions. An emperor needs to be able to chop off heads as easily as a dog sits down. He must be alert to plots even within his family and be prepared to execute those closest to him. The blessed Claudius, for example, killed his father-in-law, his two sons-in-law, his daughter's father-in-law (who was as like him as two eggs in a basket), Scribonia (his daughter's mother-in-law), his wife Messalina, and others too numerous to mention, all without a proper hearing. Yet he sits in Olympus with the other gods. You too must learn to do whatever it takes to attain such high honour.

We Romans were destined to rule the world. Other peoples can make fine bronze and marble statues or speak more eloquently or are capable of understanding the movements of the stars more accurately. The fate of the Romans is to hold supreme authority over these peoples. The ability to establish law and order and enforce peace, to be merciful to those that submit, and to crush those who are arrogant enough to oppose us, these are the special Roman skills.

But empire has made us rich. We would be foolish to imagine that we can ignore this fact in how we live today. We Romans know better than anyone how to live the good life. Whether it is relaxing in the baths or enjoying the great gladiatorial games, Romans understand how such wealth is to be put to proper use. We control our wealth; it does not control us. The great examples of Rome's early history can teach you all you need to know about the correct core attitudes you must possess if you are to succeed in life but I can tell you how to cope with the wealth and glory that such success will inevitably bring.

We should pray too for struggles in life. Prosperity can be won by any person, whatever their background. It is only great men who are able to cope with the disasters and terrors that habitually affect human life. If you live comfortably and in prosperity, and never suffer the merest hint of mental distress, then you will have experienced only half of what life has to offer. You may think you are great, and this book may even help make you become so, but how can anyone tell, if fortune offers you no opportunity of showing your virtue? It would be like entering the arena at the Olympic games alone and with no opponent to face. You would win the crown but not the victory, let alone the glory. A man cannot know himself without putting himself to the test. Otherwise he will never know what he is capable of. You should be prepared to expose yourself willingly to risks and dangers to be able to better know yourself. Truly great people love a fight just as brave soldiers do in war. Like the prize gladiator, Triumphus, who fought during the time of the emperor Tiberius, you should complain when you have no opponents left who are your equal: 'Now there is no chance for glory left,' he bemoaned. Greatness needs risk and thinks only of its ends, not what it will suffer en route to achieving them. Just as soldiers pride themselves on their wounds, showing off their blood-spattered breastplates, you too must wear the scars of life with joy. Only then will your life of leisure have worth and feel like it has been deserved. Only then will you be honoured for the glory you have won. Only then will you have released your inner Roman.

·· COMMENTARY ··

 Rome was founded, according to legend, on 21 April 753 BC. For the next two and a half centuries it was governed by kings until, in about 509 BC, an uprising led to the overthrow of Tarquin the Proud and the establishment of a republic. Many of the details of this period are hard to establish with any certainty and were only recorded centuries later. We should therefore take the stories of Roman heroism with a pinch of salt. One fact that Falx conveniently forgets to mention is that Rome was probably captured by Porsena, the king of the nearby city of Clusium. But true or not, the Romans liked to tell themselves these stories because they felt they were redolent of the kind of attitude that had enabled Rome to conquer the many surrounding towns and peoples and slowly establish its authority in Latium, the area around Rome itself, and then the wider Italian peninsula.

The conquest of Italy was just the beginning. By the time of the fall of the republic in 27 BC, when Julius Caesar's adopted son Octavian became the first emperor (known as Augustus), Rome had control of territories stretching from the English Channel to the Black Sea, and from North Africa to Syria. Its empire contained a population of some sixty to seventy million people and it covered an area twenty times the size of the modern UK. By any standards, but especially those of a pre-industrial society, this was a colossal state.

But success brought riches, and the massive influx of wealth, power and people into Rome utterly transformed what had begun as a traditional agrarian society. The emperors had vast sums to lavish on building programmes, on huge public shows, on free food handouts, and on providing leisure facilities such as the great imperial baths (those of Caracalla are the best surviving example). What it meant to be a Roman was itself transformed. Now the Romans had to learn how to cope with this influx of luxury and leisure without compromising the military ideals that had won them the empire in the first place. It was not always an easy balancing act. Many traditionalists roundly condemned the new 'softness' they found in Roman society. But most Romans seem to have been happy to enjoy the fruits of success wherever and whenever they could. The heroic tales of the likes of Mucius Scaevola, 'the left-handed one', and the ultimate in tough-love fatherhood, Brutus, came to horrify as much as they inspired.

The story of Mucius is from Livy's *History of Rome* (1.2.12–13), while that of Horatius Cocles can be found in Polybius's *History* (6.64–5). Livy (2.3) describes Brutus's execution of his own sons. The account of Falx's successful slave, called 'the farmer', is based on the inscription *CIL* 11.600. The definition of piety comes from Cicero's *On Rhetorical Invention* 2.22.66. The standard, narrow range of virtues that a woman was thought to be able to possess or have the opportunity to display can be neatly found in the funerary inscription *CIL* 6.10230. Falx's debt to his father is based on that of Horace (*Satire* 1.6.65–88). The list of dreadful acts allegedly carried out by the emperor Claudius can be found in Seneca's satirical account of the deified emperor's trial in Mount Olympus for his misdeeds, *The Pumpkinification of Claudius*. Virgil famously lists the Roman USPs in his *Aeneid* (6.847–53), while Seneca (*On Providence* 4) argues that we need bad things to happen to us in life if we are to experience it fully. He himself got his wish as he was forced to commit suicide by the emperor Nero, whose tutor he had once been.

CHAPTER II

CONQUER YOUR EMOTIONS

O NLY WHEN YOU HAVE LEARNED how to think like a Roman can you start to live like one. Rome's success stems from its military success. Military success can only happen if there is discipline. You must first acquire a backbone of inner toughness if you are to improve your barbarian ways.

Victory in war does not depend simply on the number of troops a general has at his disposal or on the courage of the troops themselves. Only skill and discipline can ensure success. The Romans owe their conquest of the world to their continual military training, to the meticulous observance of discipline in their camps, and to their scrupulous attention to the details of the arts of war. Without these, what chance would the small number of Roman legionaries have had against the vast ranks of the Gauls? Or how could the average Roman soldier, less than six Roman feet tall, cope with huge blonde-haired German tribesmen? The Spanish outnumbered us and were physically stronger too. We were always inferior to the Egyptians in both wealth and trickery. As for the Greeks, we could never match them in knowledge. Against all these disadvantages, the Romans made sure they recruited only the best troops and then took unusual care in their military training. They understood the importance of toughening up their soldiers by endless practice in all the manoeuvres they would ever need on the battlefield. The courage of a soldier is heightened by his professional knowledge. He then yearns to have the opportunity to execute what he has been perfectly taught. Because a general gives the most dangerous jobs to the best soldiers – whether it is ambushing by night, attacking well-defended positions or scouting behind enemy lines – a soldier who is ordered to do such difficult tasks takes it as the highest compliment. Like the Spartans, who test their sons' mettle by publicly flogging them, generals exhort their troops to endure their wounds bravely and offer their torn flesh to receive yet more punishment. A handful of such battle-hardened men will always defeat far larger armies of raw and undisciplined troops. The recruit turns pale at the thought of being wounded, whereas the veteran knows that losing blood is part of the price of victory.

The Roman empire was not won by chance. Romans understand that idleness is the enemy of discipline. Even during long periods of peace, they never stop their military exercises. And those exercises are every bit as demanding as the real thing. Every soldier is exercised vigorously every day, with the result that when war does break out then nobody notices any change. The troops can easily cope with the fatigue of forced marches and of prolonged fighting. Hand-to-hand combat holds no fear for them because their daily exercise could more accurately be described as 'bloody training sessions'.

Their fitness and training also means that the enemy cannot surprise them with sudden counter-attacks. As soon as the Roman troops have marched into foreign territory, they avoid contact with the enemy until they have fortified their camp. They level out the ground if it is uneven and then a great throng of carpenters raises a fence. Towers are put up equally spaced apart and between them are positioned the engines for throwing arrows, stones and other missiles. A ditch is then dug around the whole perimeter, measuring four cubits in both width and depth. They also erect four gates, one on each side of the square camp, which are made large enough for bringing in cattle and also for troops to leave quickly. Within the walls, the camp is divided into streets, with the commander's tent in the middle. Sections are also ascribed for the men's tents, for the smiths and for the storage of supplies.

The troops are organised into small companies. Each company keeps its own affairs in order, in terms of supplies of wood, water and corn. They do everything as a unit. They take their meals together, and arrange their sleep so that they take it in turns to keep watch. Everything is marked by the sound of the trumpet. Every day the general hands down the watchword in order to prevent any of the enemy from entering the fort. He then gives other orders that are handed down via the superior officers to the centurions and then to the troops. This line of command controls everything the men do and can turn them about in an instant if required during a mission.

When the Romans go into battle they plan for every contingency. Every decision is executed promptly. This means that they almost never make mistakes and if they do they are quickly able to correct them because they have a back-up plan in place. They do not worry if they get things wrong so long as the mistakes happen because a strategy has not worked as they had hoped. They would much prefer to fail like that than be successful as a result of some lucky act of ill-considered rashness. Hot-headedness needs good fortune, planning does not. If you have planned well, but then fail, you will always have the comfort of knowing that you had tried hard to prevent it.

When they carry out their military training, the Romans set out to strengthen the soldier's very soul, not just his body. Soldiers are also toughened up for war by fear. The law dictates that any legionaries who desert their ranks on the battlefield shall be executed. Laziness can also be punished by death. A Roman general is even more severe than the law, which he enforces on all troops equally and with a rigour that leaves them in no doubt as to their fate should they fall short of the high standards expected of them. But with the rod, goes the carrot. The generals bestow colossal rewards on soldiers who carry out acts of conspicuous bravery. It all means that the troops are in the total control of their commanders. In battle the whole army moves as if it were a single body, so rapidly can it manoeuvre and so quickly does it respond to orders. Whatever they do is done immediately and is completed with great speed. Whatever they have to suffer they do with the greatest patience and forbearance. The Roman conquests have therefore all been well deserved and none have relied on luck. Given the level of planning, organisation and, above all, discipline, is it any wonder that our empire stretches from the Euphrates in the East to the Ocean in the West, from the fertile lands of Libya in the South to the Rhine and Danube in the North? It would be fair to say that the size of our empire reflects the greatness of the Romans themselves.

It is rare for Roman soldiers to fail to live up to these high standards. As I say, any lapse in discipline is harshly punished. A soldier who does something in battle against orders is executed even if his actions are successful. Even more draconian treatment is traditionally reserved for troops who fail to show proper Roman discipline in battle: they are decimated. A cohort will be chosen for the punishment and it will then be divided into groups of ten men. Each group then draws lots to decide which of them shall be executed by the other nine. The victim, who could be of any rank and is selected regardless of his level of guilt, is then clubbed or stoned to death by his comrades. The surviving soldiers might also be fed less palatable rations for a while, such as barley instead of the usual wheat. They might even be forced to pitch their tents outside the protective fence of the camp as a sign of their distance from the army itself.

The first decimation occurred a generation after the removal of the kings, when the young republic found itself at war with the Volsci. The Roman soldiers seemed more willing to be defeated than to be victorious. They despised their aristocratic commanders, who hated them in return. No matter how savagely the generals treated the Roman men, so deep was the troops' opposition that they acted with the utmost laziness and obstinacy in all that they did. If told to advance rapidly they would slow down; if ordered to work, they would relax. It was a case of donkeys led by lions!

When drawn up into battle order, they fled the Volsci and sought the safety of their camp. They refused to make a stand until they could see the enemy actually advancing on their fortifications and slaughtering those at the rear who had failed to make it back to the camp. This forced them to fight, with the result that the enemy were forced back from the perimeter fence just as they were about to grasp victory. Disaster had been averted but it was clear that the only thing the Roman soldiers cared about was the protection of the camp. They had no shame about letting Rome down.

One commander, Appius, refused to give up on this ill-disciplined rabble. He wanted to call an assembly of the men and rage at them but all the other officers warned him not to try to assert his authority when his ability to command depended on the troops' goodwill and willingness to obey. They said that the men would refuse to simply be harangued. Appius decided to back down for the moment, deciding that the troops would only be delaying their inevitable comeuppance. Instead, he ordered the army to march out of the camp the following day. The Volsci immediately attacked the rear of the Roman column and confusion soon spread right through the Roman ranks. The panic was so great that it was impossible to hear commands or form a line and even the Roman standards were lost. Everyone tried to flee, scrambling over the bodies of their dead comrades and their discarded weapons in order to make it back to the camp.

When at last the Roman soldiers had been collected together, Appius called an assembly and laid into the men savagely. What kind of army were they, he said, that had no discipline and had deserted its standards? Each soldier who had thrown away his weapons or his standards and any officer who had deserted his post was beaten and then beheaded. Of the remainder, one in ten was chosen by lot for punishment in the manner described above. Never again would a Roman army go into battle without the protection of discipline and order.

The success that such a disciplined army inevitably won brought with it a new type of danger: luxury. As the Romans conquered so they grew rich and able to afford all kinds of extravagance both in dress and in food. Instead of simple fare on their plates, the people now indulged in fine dainties. As Cato the Elder said, how can a city continue to exist in security when a highly prized fish is selling for more than an ox? But no one would listen to him. As he also said, it is hard to talk to a belly with no ears. All that people cared about were what delicacies would next pass their lips.

And as Cato had warned so it came to pass. This extravagance did indeed begin to infect the army. When Scipio the Younger arrived at one camp he found all manner of licentiousness and luxury that could only ever result in disorder among the troops. He issued orders for all the soothsayers and prostitutes to be driven out of the camp. He even commanded that the only utensils a soldier should be allowed to possess were a pot, a fork and an earthenware drinking cup. He banned bathing and said that men should only rub themselves down, not receive massages from others. The troops were forbidden from reclining at dinner, which he ordered should consist only of bread, porridge or boiled meat. The only luxury he allowed the men was that each could keep a silver tankard of not more than two pounds in weight if they so wished. He himself went about wearing a plain black cloak, saying that he was in mourning for the army's lost honour.

Nothing is so perilous as luxury. It softens a man's feet to bathe them regularly and for them to walk on floors with heating beneath. Such a man cannot bear to wear the hobnailed army boot at all, let alone march for thirty miles a day. All excesses are damaging but excess of comfort is the worst. It addles the brain. It blurs the truth of manhood with the soft lies of vanity.

Luxury weakens the spirit too. You must harden your heart along with your feet. How can you expect to take the tough decisions necessary to be a success unless you learn to control your emotions? Conquering others and making them your subjects is not for the faint-hearted. Giving way to inner emotions can only prevent you from carrying out your duty. I remember sacking a city once. Those inside had resisted us and so deserved their terrible fate. Thousands of us armed men burst through the walls. Neither status nor age protected anyone inside. We killed without distinction. Whenever a young woman or a handsome youth was captured, they were torn to pieces in the violent struggle of their captors to own them. Some soldiers tortured inhabitants to try to force them to reveal where they had hidden their money and valuables. Everywhere lay the horrors of war: the rape of virgin girls and boys, children torn from their parents' arms, mothers subjected to the will of the victors, temples and homes pillaged, bloodshed and fire. In short, everywhere lay arms and corpses, gore and grief.

In the chaos, there was no crime that was held to be unlawful. Flames raced through the houses and temples, the crash of falling roofs filled the air, and the single sound made up of many cries pierced the ear. Some inhabitants tried to flee in blind panic, while others clung to their loved ones in a last embrace before being driven off in chains to a life of slavery. Then there was the foolish mother who desperately tried to keep her child with her before being beaten off by a soldier. You could make up any horror story you like and it would not be worse than the truth.

The end justified these means. After this brief period of pain, the inhabitants of the city became subject to Roman rule and all its many benefits. A short war brought a lasting peace. Peace brought trade. Trade brought wealth. Soon the city prospered and when I happened to return to it some years later it was booming, with a fine new amphitheatre almost completed, paved streets and an impressive forum decorated with statues of the emperor.

It is, of course, an inevitable rule of nature that she

will sometimes choose to withdraw her favour in one region or another and the crops will fail as a result. Then you will encounter many gruesome scenes as the peasants and townsfolk go hungry. Emotions must also be controlled when dealing with these starving people. I remember once passing through the province of Cappadocia during a time of famine. Countless people lay dying in the cities, and even more so in the countryside. The price of wheat shot up and I heard tales of 2,500 sesterces being paid for a single measure. At first, people sold off their dearest possessions, although with everyone trying to do this the price for valuables dropped precipitously. The poor then resorted to eating anything that might provide a little nourishment. They ate grass and loaves made from acorns, while many damaged their health and died from chewing small wisps of hay and recklessly eating certain pernicious herbs. Many tried to flee to neighbouring areas hearing rumours that the crops had not failed there, but they lacked the provisions to sustain them on the journey and so often fell by the wayside. Others made endless sacrifices to the gods, hoping to persuade them to send help. Some well-born ladies were driven by their hunger to shameless acts of begging in the marketplace. Other women turned to even worse behaviour, selling their bodies to soldiers or indeed anyone for a morsel of bread. Many parents sold off one or more of their children into slavery.

When the famine was in its early days, the wealthy were generous and gave out subsidised corn. Hunger makes men liars, as the saying goes, and people invented all kinds of exaggerated tales in order to try to persuade the rich to help them, which to begin with they did. But as the famine spread, the wealthy were amazed at the multitude of beggars and, after giving countless gifts of help, adopted a hard and pitiless frame of mind. If they were to survive they had to keep what they had for themselves. Some of the starving grew angry with the town's officials and protested at the lack of food. They accused the city's wealthiest citizens of hoarding food in their barns in order to drive up the price and so make a killing. The officials responded by withdrawing to their country estates for safety, where they had sufficient reserves stored up to maintain their own households. The rest slowly starved. Their skin shrivelled and turned black, their faces became fixed with a dreadful sort of insane stare. Some wasted away like ghosts, others cried out for scraps of food right up to the end. The dead lay in the marketplace and alleys where they were stripped naked of anything that could be sold to buy food. People no longer had the means or the energy to give their kin a proper burial and, instead, the bodies lay unburied for many days, rotting into the most piteous spectacle. Some of the corpses were eaten by dogs, and for this reason those who were alive turned to killing the dogs, for fear lest the animals became mad and started hunting people for food. Many ate the dogs. Rumours abounded of some even eating the flesh of the human dead.

It is not only to the starving poor that you must sometimes harden your heart. Within your household you must make sure that you do not fall for the wiles of women. 'Don't trust a woman till she's dead,' as the saying goes. Nor should you believe the tears of an angry wife. When a woman weeps, she fills the tears with many ambushes. The overly generous husband will soon find himself controlled by his wife when it should be the other way round. Likewise with slaves: as the proverb goes, 'the clever slave has a share in power'. If you allow your slaves to work on your weaker side you will soon find yourself running around after them.

Let me reiterate the lessons I taught you in my manual on slave management. You must maintain order at all costs and not be afraid to assert your authority from time to time. Punish your slave if he gives you a cheeky or disrespectful look. If you find the thought of carrying out the punishment yourself distasteful then call in the municipal contractors to do it for you. Their rates are very reasonable, only four sesterces per flogging, and they even bring ropes and a gibbet with them. Just be careful not to punish excessively. Some masters engage in all kinds of overreaction against slaves, particularly returned runaways whom they bind in chains, flog mercilessly, or even mutilate by cutting off their hands and feet. By letting anger take control of them, these people are themselves losing control. Punishment must be meted out according to what is deserved or dictated by law. If it is appropriate for a slave to be punished by being sent to the mines then you should feel no remorse for the terrible hardships they are forced to endure there.

Rationality must always rule the head. You must sell off slaves that are unproductive. If they are sick, give them a chance to recover and then get rid of them. You must manage your portfolio to ensure that there is a balance between home-bred slaves and those who have been bought in, between young slaves in need of training and the old who can provide it. At times that will necessitate making tough choices, such as selling off the children of slave couples in your service. While that should be avoided if at all possible – it generates much ill feeling – there are times when it makes clear sense to do so and sense must prevail.

Slaves have to learn to control their emotions the hard way. They dare not reveal what they are really thinking to their master. That is why fables were invented. Slaves could not express themselves openly and so put across their feelings in interesting stories, thereby avoiding retribution. These fables did not originate with Aesop, as is commonly thought, even though they are best known by his name – Hesiod seems to have been the first to write them. They are particularly pleasing to simple, uneducated folk, who take fiction at face value and agree with whatever entertains them. That is how Menenius Agrippa is said to have used the fable of the limbs' quarrel with the belly in order to reconcile the plebs to the Roman aristocracy. The plebs had complained that the rich were taking everything for themselves but were not productive. The fable showed them that even though the legs and arms did all the work it was the belly that gave them the energy to do so. Each element needed every other.

We free people (any slaves reading this may do so in preparation for their longed-for future freedom) do not have the benefits of the external constraints imposed by a stern master. We must learn to control our own emotions. To begin with, it is easier to refuse entry to excessive emotions than to control them when they are already within us. Like a disease, once such feelings have you in their grip they are often stronger than your ability to restrain them. Second, you should understand that the mind can only remain in control so long as it is kept separate from the emotions. Once it has been infected by passion, the head is unable to stop people from doing things that they would not have done if their brains were in control. They become the slaves of the emotions. The individual in such a state is like a slave that has been thrown off the Tarpeian Rock: he has no control of his body and cannot prevent what is inevitably going to happen. So if the mind plunges into anger, love or some other passion, it has no power to arrest its fall.

The best course of action is to reject anger the moment it rears its head. Once rage has got hold of us it is difficult to get back on the straight road. The enemy, I repeat, must be stopped at the very gates: once he has entered the citadel of the head, he will have no respect for his captives. I aim higher than such an existence. I was born to a greater destiny than to be a mere slave of my body. Instead, I treat it as a kind of buffer zone that may receive blows and wounds, but I do not allow any of them to penetrate through to my soul. My body lives surrounded by dangers, but whatever happens, my soul lives free. Never do I let my physical desires lead me to lie or adopt a position which is unworthy of an honourable man. If it becomes necessary, I shall sever my connection with my body and die. In the meantime, while I am forced to cohabit with it, it is not a relationship between equals. The soul is the judge of all disputes.

To despise our bodies is a sure road to personal freedom. To accept the blows of fate is another. Disasters are a normal part of life. The true individual will be able to shrug off the problems that inevitably will come his way as he progresses through life's course. There is no virtue in living well when times are easy. As the saying goes, 'anyone can be a pilot in a calm sea'. We must limit our compassion for those who overreact to such difficulties. I remember there was once a food shortage in Rome. Not a famine, you understand, simply that a few grain ships had been delayed by adverse winds, but this was enough to raise rumours of supplies running out and caused many to hoard stocks, thereby exacerbating the problem. People were ill at ease and could be seen gathering together in huddles to discuss plans to overthrow the state and even went about at night posting up notices complaining about the government, all of which contributed to the general commotion in the city. The emperor rightly refused to stand for such behaviour. Rewards were offered for information about the ringleaders and informants soon came forward. In the end, the unrest continued until the grain ships finally docked in Ostia and the emperor put on some gladiatorial shows, ostensibly to celebrate their arrival but in reality to try to shake the plebs out of their sullen mood.

Naturally, there are crisis situations when people should be helped. During the time of the emperor Tiberius, for example, a cheaply constructed wooden amphitheatre at the town of Fidenae near Rome, which had been erected by an unscrupulous local business-man, called Atilius, to host a gladiatorial show, collapsed during the performance. Fifty thousand had crammed into the flimsy structure, with people's desire to watch the fights only fanned by the emperor's previous ban on gladiatorial shows. The surviving relatives were left to quarrel over the mutilated corpses whose identity was indeterminable, and as many as twenty thousand died. Countless others were wounded and the great families threw open their houses to help them: dressings and doctors were supplied to all-comers, regardless of their status. Longer-term help was also given to all spectators at such games. The problem had been caused by a greedy pleb so the senate decreed that in the future only those eligible for the equestrian class should be allowed to put on games, since their high status should make them less susceptible to such common avarice. It was also determined that all amphitheatres should now be built with solid foundations.

The eruption of Vesuvius, which destroyed the towns of Pompeii and Herculaneum, provided a fine example for the best individuals to show off their inner qualities. The elder Pliny was at the time in command of the fleet in nearby Misenum. He had been taking the sun, before having a cold bath and then lunching, and was working at his books when the eruption took place. Inspired by his intellectual curiosity, he went off to investigate. But then he received a letter from a noblewoman called Rectina, whose house sat at the foot of the mountain and was trapped; escape was possible only by boat. Terrified, she implored him to rescue her from her fate. Immediately, he changed his plans and what he had begun in a spirit of inquiry he completed as a hero.

He gave orders for the warships to be launched and went on board himself with the intention of bringing help to many more people besides Rectina, for this lovely stretch of coast was thickly populated. Tragically, this great man was struck down by falling debris as his boat approached the coast.

His nephew, the younger Pliny, stayed back at the house with his mother. A friend of his uncle's from Spain urged them to escape, claiming that it would be what the older Pliny would want. Initially, the younger man refused, saying bravely that he would not think of considering his own safety as long as he was uncertain of his uncle's. His mother begged him to leave: 'a young man might escape,' she said, 'whereas I am old and slow and could die in peace so long as I have not been the cause of my son's death too.' Still he refused. But once it seemed that the house itself was about to collapse, he decided to leave but took her with him, dragging her along to move more quickly. Once they were away from the buildings they stopped and, looking back, could see the earth moving and the sea being sucked away, as if it were being forced back by the earthquake, with the result that many sea creatures were left stranded on dry land.

Of course, these details of minor disasters are not important enough for history. The only reason I am telling them to you is to highlight the benefit that disasters can bring. When there is panic, when cities collapse or are buried, when populations are crushed and the earth shakes, what wonder is it that most minds are gripped by fear? Terror disturbs many so much that it carries them off into insanity. Or it sends them off into the arms of superstition. You will never find more prophecies of doom than when fear mixed with religion strikes the minds of men who should know better. It is not easy to keep your wits about you during great distress. Only the most stable can keep control of their emotions. You should not be afraid to expose yourself to stress so that you can learn the better to cope with it. In the same way that the bodies of sailors are hardened by endurance of the sea, the hands of farmers toughened by manual labour, and the arms of soldiers made strong by hurling javelins, so you can build up your mind to be able to endure the most dramatic misfortunes. You might even learn to laugh off such danger. A friend of mine was once on a sea voyage when a huge storm blew up. His slaves wept in terror at the thought of what might happen. 'Don't cry,' he consoled them, 'I have freed you all in my will.'

Death will visit you soon enough. Or a member of your family will be struck down. You should save your compassion for those who are dear to you. Some years ago I lost a dear son, Marcus, a boy of whom I had formed the highest expectations and in whom I had placed all the hopes for my old age. For me, his death was such a blow that for a long time after nothing could bring me any happiness. It was like losing one of my two eyes. I have no desire to flaunt my woes before you in public but you could do well to learn from my self-control. Even now I cannot forget the charm of his face, the sweetness of his lisping speech, his first flashes of promise, and his powerful mind. I was everything to him

as he was to me. He devoted all his love to me, prefer-
ring me to his nanny, his grandmother, his siblings and
even his dear mother. I swear by my own sad heart, by
his departed spirit, and by the deity at his shrine where I
pray each day, that I saw in him a talent I have never seen
anywhere else. His speed at learning, his spontaneous
ability to work, his warm and pious nature should all
have filled me with dread. For it is commonly observed
that those who ripen early die young. There seems to
be some malign influence in the world that delights in
cutting down those with the greatest promise and refuses
to allow our joys to exceed the limit allotted to mortals.

He possessed every advantage. His Latin was fine and
he pronounced every Greek letter perfectly, speaking it
as if it were his mother tongue. In all his actions there
was the promise of greater things to come. He had the
finer qualities: courage, dignity and the strength to put
up with both fear and pain. What bravery he showed
during his eight-month-long illness. His doctors mar-
velled at his tenacity. How he consoled me during his last
moments. Even when he became delirious, his thoughts
turned to his lessons and what he had learned at school.
When he died, my hopes died with him. I embraced
his cold, pale body at a time when he should have been
setting off on a career that would have led to the highest
offices of state.

I hope my endurance may prove worthy of him in my
remaining years. We must find some purpose in life in
order to make it tolerable. The wise have taught that literature alone can provide true solace in adversity and so
I turned to writing. Women too can treat the hardships

that fortune sends our way as a means of displaying their inner worth. I am reminded of the story of Arria, whose husband, Caecina Paetus, was ill at the same time as her son. Neither was expected to recover. The boy died – he was of exceptional beauty and modesty and his parents loved him for all sorts of reasons besides his being their son. Arria made arrangements for the boy's funeral and then attended it without telling her husband. When Caecina asked, she even pretended the boy was still alive and feeling better, claiming he had rested well and had recovered his appetite. Whenever she felt overwhelmed by her grief she left the room to cry. Once she had recovered her composure she came back into the room completely calm, as if she had simply left her grief outside. What greater example can there be of female glory: to continue to act like a mother after she had lost her son?

Why is it that grief agitates us so deeply? Why should we be surprised that fortune has dealt with us so? You would imagine that all hearts would lose their sensitivity and learn to regard everything as ephemeral and unimportant. We must console ourselves with the thought that the dead are spared the pain of living in the present age. It is dreadful to lose your children. It is even worse to suffer the world as it is. One event that did indeed console me occurred during a voyage from visiting my estates in Africa. I sailed past Carthage and Syracuse, cities that at one time flourished but now are subject to Rome. We feel so outraged if a single individual within our family dies yet so many thousands perished in the capture of these once great cities. We are all born as mere mortals. It takes only a single blow to kill a man and how many thousands of fine Romans have fallen in the conquest of its empire. How can we grieve excessively for the loss of one child? If poor Marcus had not died then, he would still have had to die in the future. I decided to rejoice in what life he did have and remember who I am: a Falx. A man accustomed to instruct and offer guidance. It was time for me to act according to the advice I give others.

Time softens all sorrow. You can reach the same end earlier if you accept that that is where you are heading. I do not know if the dead retain any consciousness in the world below, but such was his love for me and his dutiful affection for all his family, that Marcus certainly would not have wanted me to carry on grieving. He would have wanted me to bear my loss with a noble dignity that would enhance an already great family name. For just as all the world's rivers do not change the taste of the sea, so hard times do not affect the mind of the brave. The mind of a real man maintains its balance and keeps control over the emotions that fortune's assaults generate. It is undoubtedly as easy to hate fortune as it is hard to bear her blows, but there is nothing left she can do to me.

·· COMMENTARY ··

Rome's military discipline undoubtedly contributed greatly to its success. This was recognised both by Roman authors and by those conquered by Rome. The Romans' success certainly could not simply be ascribed to their physical size. Recruits were measured to check that they were tall enough but how tall that was is not clear. Vegetius gives a minimum height restriction of six Roman feet, equivalent to about 5 feet 10 inches or 178 cm, for auxiliary cavalry and the first cohort of troops, but these are clearly elite soldiers and not representative of the average. The minimum height for more normal recruits attested to in other imperial regulations suggests 5 feet 7 inches in Roman terms, or 5 feet 5 inches/165 cm, although the evidence is not entirely consistent. There is a considerable range of estimates for how tall the average Roman male was, but something around 5 feet 4 inches to 5 feet 7 inches (162–171 cm) seems most plausible. It is probably wrong to look for an exact figure being meticulously adhered to by recruiting sergeants. Rather the aim was to take men who were of above average height and so, in that sense, had impressive statures. The degree to which this was followed doubtless depended on how great was the need to recruit troops or on how many volunteers came forward. In the peaceful days of the empire, being a legionary was an attractive career, with security of pay and a lump sum on retirement. Recruiters could then be more choosy about their selections. During a war or after a period of plague recruits were harder to come by and height restrictions were probably interpreted more loosely.

Livy (*History of Rome* 2.59) has an account of the first decimation in 471 BC. The number killed will have varied but if applied only to a cohort of about five hundred men then the number killed will have been about fifty: large, but still a tiny percentage of the army as a whole.

By the late republic the practice had fallen out of use, although it was revived by Crassus in 71 BC when Rome was suffering the great embarrassment of struggling to defeat the slave army of Spartacus. Julius Caesar threatened the ninth legion with decimation during the civil war between him and Pompey but did not carry it out.

On Roman military discipline, see Vegetius *Military Matters* 1.1 and, for a Romano-Jewish view, Josephus *The Jewish War* 3.71–97. Details of the sacking of a city can be found in Tacitus's account of the destruction of Cremona by Vespasian's forces in the civil war of AD 69 (*Histories* 3.33–4). Sallust (*Catiline Conspiracy* 51.9) and Quintilian (*Institutes of Oratory* 8.3.67–70) describe the hackneyed speeches that orators gave in which they dwell on the details of a fallen city, and even suggest that it was acceptable to make bits up. This implies both that the Romans were pretty hard-hearted about such accounts but also that it was still possible to move them if the suffering described was great enough.

The description of a famine is based on Procopius *History of the Wars* 6.20.18–33 and Eusebius *History of the Church* 9.8. On survival strategies during food shortages, including the consumption of crops not usually considered good for human consumption, see Garnsey, P., *Famine and Food Supply in the Graeco-Roman World: Responses to Risk and Crisis* (Cambridge University Press, 1988). Falx's call to control anger comes from Seneca's *On Anger* 1.7, 3.24 and 32, and his *Letters* 65.21–2. See Falx's *How to Manage Your Slaves* for details of the punishment of slaves. Phaedrus (*Fables* 3, preface) and Quintilian (*Institutes of Oratory* 5.11.19) explain the invention of fables. Dio Cassius (*History of Rome* 55.27) describes the food shortage of AD 6 in Rome, while the collapse of the amphitheatre at Fidenae can be found in Tacitus *Annals* 4.62–3. Details of the eruption of Vesuvius are in Pliny the Younger's *Letters* (6.16 and 20). Such events gave the ruling class the opportunity to promote themselves but also show that they were under pressure to act. The state's main role in disasters was simply to maintain order. See Jerry Toner, *Roman Disasters* (Polity 2013).

Low life expectancy meant that most families would have experienced death on a fairly regular basis. The account of Falx's dead son is based on Quintilian (*Institutes of Oratory* 6, preface), which gives a moving description of the death of his wife and two sons. It shows that for all their familiarity with brutality and death, the Romans were still capable of feeling and expressing strong emotions in the face of loss. Attempts at consolation for such grief can be found in Cicero's *Letters to Friends* 4.5 and Seneca *On Providence* 2, while the story of Arria is in Pliny the Younger *Letters* (3.16). Another interesting example of such consolation literature can be found in the recently discovered text by the medical writer Galen. Found in a Greek monastery and entitled *On the Avoidance of Grief*, it describes how Galen coped with the destruction of most of his vast library and of his stores of medicines and medical instruments in a fire in Rome in AD 192.

CHAPTER III

CLIMB THE OILY POLE

ONE SUNNY DAY IN ROME, I lunched with two friends from my youth whom I had not seen for some years and naturally we wanted to hear how each other's lives had unfolded. When we were young our families all had roughly the same standing in society. Not any more. One had lost everything in a series of reckless trading enterprises, the other had lived the quiet life on the family estates, while I had enjoyed an illustrious career in the army and in the service of our emperor. I now stood well above them both in wealth, possessions and status. You too should focus on trying to raise yourself up in society. If there is one thing you will need to achieve this it is money. Whether your goal is land, slaves or political office, all will require significant sums of cash to acquire. If you wish to realise the ultimate ambition of becoming a senator, you will need to make yourself a sesterce-millionaire; if you wish to become a member of the equestrian class you will need four hundred thousand. Whatever the level of your aspirations, I shall describe what options you have to make yourself and your family better off and thereby to improve your rank in society.

Let me begin at the bottom. It is vital for you to understand which trades are suitable for a gentleman and which ones are unacceptably vulgar. The first type of undesirable job is that of tax-gatherer. These people not only have to deal with the common herd but prey on them too. The next type of vulgar livelihood is hiring yourself out for paid employment, especially when it involves only manual labour. The wage these people receive is simply a symbol of their virtual slavery. We must also consider as plebeian those who are involved in the retail trade. They buy from wholesalers then sell the goods immediately to members of the public for a profit. They would make no money without misrepresenting the true value of what they are selling and there is no worse act than lying.

Next come those engaged in skilled labour. There is nothing gentlemanly about a workshop. The least respectable trades are those that cater for the physical and sensual pleasures of others: fishermen and fishmongers, butchers, cooks and chicken-sellers. You can add to these perfumers, dancers and all celebrities.

Of all the many places in the empire I have visited, Alexandria in Egypt was the place where the skills of these artisan sorts were most on display. The inhabitants of that city have a dreadful reputation and rightly so: they are a highly volatile, deceitful and aggressive people. But their city is prosperous and almost nobody is idle. Some work as glass-blowers, others as paper-makers or linen-weavers, or craftsmen of one kind or another. Even the lame, the blind and the eunuchs have their occupations and not even those whose hands are crippled sit about idly. Their only god is money, which they love with a fervour regardless of their religion.

You can get some idea of the reason why learning a trade is so important to ordinary people when you compare what artisans earn with the wages of simple manual workers. An unskilled labourer earns about one sesterce per day, whether they are working on a farm, driving mules or emptying out the sewers. By contrast, those who work as carpenters or stone masons earn twice as much – yes, a full two sesterces a day – while those in possession of a skill that a man of means might appreciate, such as wall-painting or mosaic-laying, can earn multiples of these figures. Beware, though, of a man who has abandoned the craft of his ancestors for a less honourable but more lucrative profession. What does it say of a man if his forefathers were generals and he reduces himself to singing or playing the pipes? I am not saying that someone who continues to work in the same dishonourable profession as his ancestors should be blamed for it. Indeed, there is something praiseworthy about those who are content with their lot and do not try to rise above their station. Not everyone can have a superior profession to that of their father. That way, there would be nobody left to carry out the menial tasks that society needs to be performed.

Professions which require either a higher level of intelligence or which serve the public good – such as medicine, architecture and teaching – are all fit and proper for those of a modest social level. Trade is vulgar if it is done on a small scale. If it is executed on a large scale, importing great quantities of materials from all over the globe and then distributing them widely without the fraudulent misrepresentation of retail, then we should not look down on it too harshly. In fact, it can even merit the utmost respect if those who have engaged in the practice turn their attention away from the markets and reinvest their fortunes in a country estate. But of all the occupations a man can have, none is better than farming. No work is more profitable, none more delightful, none more becoming to a free man.

When it comes to money, you will find the following rules useful:

- Do not spend more than you have coming in, otherwise your possessions will soon be eaten up. Instead, you should make sure that you have a surplus of income and add some of it to your capital so that you have protection against the possibility of an accident, a disaster or commercial losses.

- When investing, only put money into what you understand. Do not buy an estate if you know nothing of farming or do not have the capital to develop it. Do not buy scattered estates that you cannot hope to oversee. It is like the greedy man who eats more than he is capable of digesting and then vomits it up rather than gaining any nourishment from it.

- When it comes to spending money, avoid sordid behaviour such as refusing to help relatives or friends or former slaves. Nor should you buy only the bare essentials of life. But you must not over-spend on satisfying your lusts or on expenditure that oversteps the mark of a person of your station in society. Only kings need jewels and only scholars need books.

- In business, you be must alert to those whose reputation precedes them. If you hear they have used false weights when measuring out their produce or have slapped or insulted their customers then avoid having dealings with them.

It is your duty to run your household at a profit, so long as this is achieved by honourable means. It is often necessary to weigh one priority against another. We might have to ask whether it is more important to have health than wealth. Or to favour spending money on pleasure when it might be better spent on maintaining the property. When should glory be preferred to riches? Is income from urban property ever better than one received from the farm? It reminds me of that famous saying of old Cato's: when he was asked what was the most profitable feature of an estate, he replied, 'Farming cattle successfully.' What comes next? he was asked. 'Farming cattle with limited success.' And next? 'Farming cattle with very little success.' And is there a fourth? 'Farming crops,' he replied. And when his questioner asked, 'What about money-lending?' Cato replied, 'What about murder?' We should always remember that making money is a moral matter, not just a financial transaction, and should weigh up our decisions relating to the management of wealth accordingly.

Cato came to realise that agriculture was more a matter of entertainment than profit. He therefore invested his money in ventures that were less precarious. He bought ponds, hot springs, and other areas that were heavily used by clothes washers, all of which brought him large profits. Then he used to lend money in the most disreputable of all ways, by funding trade ships in the following manner: he required his borrowers to form a large company, and when there were fifty partners and as many ships for his security, he took one share in the company himself. Not wishing to get his own hands dirty or for his name to be tainted by association with trade, he was represented by a freedman of his called Quintio, who kept an eye on all the ventures in order to make sure that everything was above board. In this way, only a small part of Cato's capital was ever at risk on a single voyage and he reaped substantial profits from the trade as a whole.

Many fortunes have been made in business. Marcus Licinius Crassus amassed the greatest. He came from a noble background, being the son of a man who had been censor and had even enjoyed a triumph for his victory over the Lusitanians in the Iberian peninsula. But the family was not wealthy and Marcus grew up in a small house with two brothers. He developed a passion for property. He even became intimate with one of the Vestal Virgins, called Licinia, because she owned an attractive villa in the suburbs of Rome, which Crassus wanted to buy at a knock-down price. He successfully badgered her into selling the property to him but this only fed his appetite to own more. His greed began to know no bounds. Despite having no more than a modest sum of money at his disposal he managed to acquire property in the most underhand way, taking advantage of fire and war to make such calamities his greatest source of wealth.

When the dictator Sulla took control of Rome and put many of his opponents to death, Crassus bought swathes of their property on the cheap. Above all, he noticed how frequently fires broke out in Rome, now that it had grown to such a vast size. So whenever a fire broke out, he rushed to the scene and made an extremely low offer to the owners of houses in the vicinity who would often accept out of fear that the fire would spread and leave them penniless. This strategy meant that the largest part of Rome came into his possession.

His huge property empire did not mean that he lived in a palace. He owned five hundred slaves in order to develop his properties but built himself only one. He also invested widely in silver mines, agricultural land and slaves. He became so rich that he bankrolled Julius Caesar's campaign for political office. His fortune was as much as two hundred million sesterces. But in the end he wished to emulate the achievements of Caesar, the man whose rise to power he had funded. He raised an army and invaded Persia but was killed in the disastrous defeat at Carrhae, where twenty thousand brave Romans died and half as many again were captured. The Persians wished to mock Crassus's great thirst for money and so they poured molten gold down the throat of his corpse.

The threat of fire means that urban property is not always a safe investment. I was once walking with my friend Julianus up to the Cispian hill when we saw that a tall apartment block, with many storeys, had caught fire.

The blaze quickly spread to the surrounding buildings and a huge conflagration erupted. As we watched the flames leaping high into the air, Julianus turned to me and said, 'City properties generate a very good income but the risks are even greater. If only some way could be devised to stop houses in Rome from so constantly catching fire then, by Jupiter, I would sell all my country estates and buy up the Esquiline!' He's right, of course. Town property can be a real headache. Two of my own shops have fallen down recently and the rest are full of cracks as if they are about to do likewise. Even the mice have moved out. Obviously, it doesn't bother a man of my great wealth or calm outlook on life, but there are many others who are constantly thrown into a panic about the collapse of their urban properties.

Lending money is always profitable. The usual rate for loans secured against Italian land is 6 per cent and for unsecured loans is 12 per cent, or 1 per cent per month. I have entered into many such contracts, including plenty in the provinces. Besides being profitable in itself such lending also allows you the opportunity to benefit your friends by sending them on commissions or selling them a share of the contract if it seems to be a particularly lucrative venture. Of course, you should be careful when involving friends in business. If they end up losing their capital because the borrower defaults they will blame you for it, however much you might have highlighted the risks to them in advance.

We lenders have such a heavy burden of worry. If you lend money to a trader you will spend anxious nights worrying about every wind that gets up or distant clap of thunder you hear, fearing lest it signifies the loss of his ships at sea. You must make your own assessments about a person's creditworthiness. As the saying goes, 'A man who is always ready to believe what he is told will never do well, in business especially.' Like a gladiator, the businessman must make his plans in the sand. It is not possible to dictate to a debtor what he should spend the money on, but it is possible to keep an eye on what he is up to and his whereabouts in case he should get into financial difficulties and think that escape is a better option than facing you in court. It is like the Aesop fable about a bat who borrowed some money to go into business with a bramble and a coot. The bat lost it all when their ship sank and she was so scared of her creditors that she only went out to search for food at night.

If one of your debtors does default you must handle him severely. Sell all of his possessions, as you are entitled to by law, even down to the very clothes he is wearing. If this still fails to raise the necessary capital to cover his debts, you should sell his children into slavery. Healthy young infants and children should fetch a decent price and the sale will also act as a warning to others who are in your debt not to consider defaulting on their obligations. Food shortages also offer considerable opportunities to make money. In such periods, the price of grain rises substantially and it is possible to make short-term unsecured loans for rates of up to 50 per cent per annum.

If you are poor and wish to become rich you will need to be smart. You should model yourself on Eros, the god of love, whose mother was Poverty and whose father was Resourcefulness. He has inherited the characteristics of both his parents. Like his mother he is needy and unkempt, has no shoes or house to live in, and sleeps rough on the street. But like his father, he is always aiming at what is beautiful, bravely hunting out the higher things in life, and always contriving some scheme or other in order to get what he wants. But you must be sure not to go beyond the bounds of decency in your search for wealth. It is all too easy to behave like a vulgar pleb. One of my freedmen once dreamed that he ate his own faeces on some bread and actually enjoyed doing so. This is what then transpired. He was lucky enough to come into an inheritance but he did so by illegal means. The fact he had enjoyed what he had done in the dream indicated that he would be receiving a benefit, but the presence of his own excrement showed that his claim would be disputed and he would fall under suspicion for his actions. His gain, in other words, was full of disgrace.

You could do worse than heeding the words of my former slave 'the farmer' who I mentioned before. He always gives his new slaves in the chain gangs a talk, telling them how they too could be as successful as him. 'Take all this as good and true advice,' he tells them, 'if you want to live really well and become free: first, show respect where it is due; next, want what's best for your master; honour your parents; earn others' trust; don't speak or listen to slander. If you don't harm or betray anyone you will lead a pleasant life, uprightly and happily, and you won't offend anyone.' If you display this kind of hard-working tenacity and deference to your superiors, you too will find that you will rise up in society.

But if you are more ambitious than 'the farmer', then

you will need to become a popular celebrity. One option is to become a gladiator. You may have no choice in the matter if you are condemned by a court to fight as a gladiator or you are a slave whose master has chosen to sell you to a gladiator school. But if you are free you may also volunteer for the shows. It has to be said that those who do volunteer generally do so for the wrong reasons – often they are former soldiers who have found it difficult to adjust to civilian life – but the very act of signing on generates a fee. Then there are the financial rewards for fighting, which will depend very much on your social status (the crowd love to see a free volunteer fight), the quality of the event and whether you are any good. The consequences of not being a good gladiator hardly need to be spelled out and so this route to success should only be chosen by those with some reasonable level of military or physical prowess. There was once a free volunteer in the town of Pompeii, called Publius Ostorius, who fought in fifty-one contests and lived to tell the tale. But even if you do have some talent, there are other considerable downsides. You are obliged to take the gladiators' oath: that you will obey your trainer absolutely and submit to be burned, flogged or killed as he so commands.

As a gladiator, you will find yourself in considerable demand if you are a nobleman or even a noblewoman and decide to volunteer. Nobility adds glamour to even the most provincial of shows. It also adds more than a whiff of scandal. A young member of the famous Gracchi family once appeared as a gladiator, which was shocking enough, but he even fought as a net-fighter, meaning that he did not wear a helmet and so his face could be seen by all. 'Why would I fight if I were a wealthy noble?' you might ask. Here you must realise that success in Rome is not simply a matter of money. Money can bring many things – power and possessions – but it cannot bring glory. Only those who have proven their manliness can achieve that. Any rich man can lounge in a bath or recline at a feast. It takes character to fight. It is also incredibly exciting. Anyone who has fought hand-to-hand in battle – when you look right into your opponent's face as you thrust your sword down into his throat – understands what is like to fight in the arena.

Success in the arena also brings great fame. You will find that everyone knows your name and will even see it scratched up in graffiti on walls. You will find mosaics celebrating the moments when you dispatched the defeated opponents who failed to win the mercy of the crowd. People will ask you for drops of blood to help cure their epilepsy or their sexual impotence. You will always find a few traditionalists who look down on you for appearing in a show but they are few and far between. Why shouldn't you want to appear in the kind of show that the emperor himself thinks worthy of spending so much money on?

There are safer options. Charioteers can earn extraordinary amounts of money. The prize money for the best races in Rome ranges from between fifteen to sixty thousand sesterces. One of my old lawyer friends complains that a charioteer can earn a hundred times the fee that he can command. The most successful driver I have come across was a man called Diocles, who came from Lusitania in Iberia. He raced for twenty-four years during the reigns of the divine emperors Hadrian and Antoninus Pius before retiring at the age of forty-two. He won a grand total of 1,462 races out of total of 4,257 runs. He had nine horses with which he had won a hundred races and one with which he had won over two hundred. His career earnings came to an astonishing 35,863,120 sesterces, which made him one of the wealthiest men in Rome.

Charioteers earn their money. Controlling a four-horse chariot is not easy. The reins of the two trace horses are bound round your body and you must use your weight to pull them into position. If you crash, you will be dragged down by these reins and trampled, unless you can manage to cut yourself free. Tactics count for everything in the race itself. If you let your horses go too soon they will use up all their energy and have nothing left for the final sprint. You will have to decide whether it is better to hold your team of horses up in order to make a late charge or whether you will try to get in front and then hold that position by sticking to the inside track and making it difficult for others to get past you. If your opponents try to draw alongside, jostle them or use your whip to try to force them back. Aim your blows at your rival horses' eyes – that often forces them back.

When there are such large sums at stake, many resort to trying to enlist the support of divine forces in their pursuit of victory. Magic spells are believed by many to have been effective in the Circus and you can learn how to direct these at your opponents. 'Help me in the races on 8 November,' you should say, 'and bind my opponents' limbs, sinews and ankles' – and here you should add the names of your rival horses and the competitor charioteers. Do not hold back, but chant something like the following: 'Torment their minds, their brains and their senses so that they don't know what they are doing, and knock out their eyes so that they cannot see where they are going, torture and kill the horses and kill them all in a crash so that not a breath is left in their bodies.'

The size of the potential gains reflects the great passion so many have for chariot racing. Perhaps two hundred and fifty thousand can spectate in the Circus Maximus and they will scream and bend double in their excitement. Often they have put large bets on the outcome, which adds to their fervour. The emperor Caligula took his obsession with the horses to a ludicrous extreme. He used to invite his favourite stallion, Charger, to dinner, where he would feed him golden barley and drink his health in wine from golden goblets. Charger's stable contained a marble stall, an ivory trough, purple blankets and a collar studded with precious stones, and the emperor even gave him a house, a team of slaves and fine furniture, so that those who he invited to dine with the horse could be more elegantly entertained. It is also said that Caligula planned to appoint the animal as a consul, a promise I have no doubt he would have carried out if he had lived longer.

However you make it, the more money you have, the higher in Roman society you will rise. If you were once a slave but acquire your freedom, you may be lucky enough to gain citizenship, with some limitations of certain offices you may hold – but your children will be full citizens. If you were born free then there is no limit to how far you can go, particularly if you have the backing of a powerful patron. You could even become a senator, like myself. The senate comprises the top six hundred in Roman society and contains only those of the highest birth. To qualify to be a senator you must be the freeborn son of a senator and have property valued at a minimum of one million sesterces. Since you are unlikely to be the son of a senator you may think that your path is blocked. But our illustrious emperor occasionally appoints individuals to the senate for some exceptional piece of good service. Each year the list of senators is updated and each individual is ranked according to their status. The emperor always tops the list, followed by the consuls and other magistrates, then the other senators according to their wealth. Those whose property has fallen below the million mark are removed.

Whether you attain the ultimate social grade or not, if you make money it is vital to display your wealth and status in an appropriate way. Assuming you manage to achieve the basic level of Roman citizen, then you will need to learn how to wear the toga. Only Roman citizens are permitted to wear this garment and you will be expected to don it for occasions such as games where the emperor himself is present or if you become a magistrate. Invest in a good-quality toga made of fine homespun wool. Make sure it is properly white. There is nothing more vulgar than the greying threadbare look of many poor artisans. Do not underestimate how heavy the toga is or how hot in summer. Be sure to keep it white by having it washed at a fullery. There, the toga will first be soaked in a vat containing a mixture of water and urine. The fullers keep piss-pots outside their premises to ensure a steady supply from passers-by. Once washed, the toga will be dried, then brushed to raise the nap of the wool, a procedure sometimes carried out with the skin of a hedgehog or a thistle. The toga will then be bleached with sulphur and finally whitened with fine white soil. It is, as you can imagine, an expensive process but it is worth it if you are to look your best.

To put it on properly, hold the toga with its curved edge at the bottom. Throw one corner over the left shoulder, then place the other part of the garment on the right shoulder. In this way your back will be covered. The toga is then passed over the front of the body, covering most of the chest and reaching down almost to the feet. The remaining corner is then tossed over the left shoulder so as to cover most of the arm. When you have finished, your right arm should be largely covered by the cloth but the weight should be supported on the left shoulder so that your right arm is free to throw off the toga at will. This will leave you free to make the necessary rhetorical gestures during the making of a speech.

If you are properly successful, you will need as large a villa as you can afford in order to entertain the most important guests you can muster. It will take a significant investment in slaves to run such a household – from cooks and cleaners to waiters and personal bodyguards. You will need to act as patron to your newly acquired household. Over time, you will acquire a set of clients – those beholden to you, many of whom will be slaves you have freed, out of generosity and in return for good service. They will be expected to visit you in the morning, daily, and will start to arrive at your door before sunrise and then wait for you to appear. Have your doorman let them enter the vestibule but you should then make a point of keeping them waiting. Their time is less important than yours and it is a reflection of your higher status that others should wait upon you. Once you have got up, dressed and breakfasted, you should have the doors to the atrium opened to allow your clients to call upon you one by one. Rank them according to their own status, with the least important being kept till last, to avoid giving any offence. It is impossible to remember all their names and you should use a slave as a name-caller so that you do not have to keep asking your clients their name, which always seems to annoy them. Invite a lucky few to accompany you on your daily business, the reward for which might be an invitation to dinner. Others might be given a small gift of money or food. Naturally, you will sometimes feel unable to face a hall crowded with clients. You should in that case escape through some concealed side door.

Holding dinner parties is a fundamental part of being a successful Roman. There are, however, many pitfalls that await a social parvenu such as yourself if you are not to appear crude and inelegant. Make sure that the seating plan reflects the status of the diners. Those of the highest rank should lie next to you, with those of the lowest status reclining the farthest away. If you are entertaining a large number of guests, you will want to have the finest dishes served to the top table. But you should be careful not to do this too obviously in case you should appear both mean and lavish at the same time. Worse still is if you apportion the wine in decanters, with the finest Falernian put in large quantities at the top table while only small quantities of wine vinegar are placed before everyone else. Too little wine is bound to breed resentment.

In smaller, more intimate dinner parties, I take care to set the same fare before all my guests. I do this even if they are freedmen. Some find it extraordinary that I should treat former slaves of mine the same as a senator. 'It must cost you a fortune!' exclaimed one of my friends. But in reality, I do not mix my genuinely important guests with freedmen. I take care only to invite social equals to dinners and at those attended by freedmen and lesser citizens they do not drink the same wine as I do normally but I drink the same as they do. Nor do I go over the top in serving a great banquet of different dishes, but keep the fare plain and simple for everyone – unless, of course, I am entertaining important guests, such as senators or close associates of the emperor, in which case I spare no expense. The best men cannot be expected to eat like paupers.

I dined recently at that same friend's house and it was pitiable to behold the scraps that were being served up at the far couches. While we were served snowy-white bread, kneaded from the finest flour, those at the bottom received lumps of mouldy crust that would easily crack your teeth. Even the slaves treated these poor wretches with utter disdain. While they couldn't do enough for us at the top couch, the slaves openly refused to get drinks for the lowest ranks. And if any diner dared to reach for the wrong bread basket and take a piece of softer bread they would quickly be forced to hand it back with a sharp, 'Keep to your own basket, if you please! Learn the colour of your bread!' Sadly, many of the great houses are full of these arrogant slaves these days. It's because they cost so much. A slave who costs thousands lets it go to his head and thinks he's worth more than a free man. I pitied my friend's poor clients who had struggled up the Esquiline hill through the hail and rain of a cold winter's day only to be treated like dogs by slaves, while we fed on lobster and asparagus.

Manners make the Roman. At the dinner, be sure to entertain the other guests with examples of your wit and charm. Wealth makes a man feel very pleased with himself and value his own opinions highly, and you should be careful not to lecture. A restrained elegance should be your aim. I had one guest recently who stuffed himself during the entire meal, then, the moment the dinner had ended, he swept up all the leftovers into his napkin to take home: teats from a sow's udder, pork ribs, and a pigeon dripping with sauce – even a meadow bird carved for two and a whole pike – all were crammed into a greasy napkin for his slave to carry home. It was most embarrassing and all the rest of us could do was recline at the table and pretend we hadn't noticed.

There is a thin line between extravagance and vulgarity. I went to a most appallingly garish affair the other evening. The host arrived late – a fault he considered more fashionable than rude – carried in a litter by liverymen decorated with metal breastplates. His favourite slave boy went before him, ready to receive his master's attentions. Another slave boy preceded the mini-procession while playing a set of pipes. Needing to relieve himself, the host then snapped his fingers at which point a young eunuch slave came forward with a silver chamber pot for him to piss into. Another brought water for him to rinse his hands, which he dried on one of the slaves' hair.

At last we reclined and two long-haired Ethiopians entered, carrying small leather bottles, such as are commonly seen in the hands of those who sprinkle sand in the arena, and poured wine upon our hands. Picking his teeth with a silver needle, the host explained his lateness. 'Friends,' he said, 'I'm afraid it was inconvenient for me to come to you because I had not finished my game of dice.' A slave brought over a terebinth table and crystal dice and he continued to play for a while. In the meantime, we poor guests were left to study the extraordinary array of delicacies being placed before us. Our spoons were made of silver and must have weighed half a pound each. Just eating was hard exercise in itself. Some glass bottles sealed with gypsum were brought in next, bearing labels that read 'Finest 100-Year-Old Falernian'. These were placed directly before us to ensure we were aware of what we were drinking. While we drank, a slave brought in a silver skeleton, which had movable joints and could be turned in any direction. For our amusement, the host, whose name is Trimalchio, threw the skeleton down upon the table and it would adopt grotesque positions.

We dined next on fattened chickens served with goose eggs capped with pastry. Trimalchio was holding his stomach in some discomfort. 'Pardon me gentlemen,' he said, 'but my guts are on strike and I've not shat for a few days. There's been such a rumbling going on you'd think a bellowing bull was in there!' He lifted up his leg and filled the room with an obscene noise and a filthy stench. 'So don't hold back if any of you need to go – there's no need to be shy. Better out than in is what I always say. Everything's ready outside – water, a commode, a slave with a sponge-stick to clean you.' We could only thank him for his kindness and consideration.

Just then a huge hog roast was placed on the table. Trimalchio examined it closely. 'What the fuck!' he shouted, 'this hog ain't been gutted! By Hercules, that cook ain't done nothing to it. Get him in here!' The poor man was dragged in. 'Strip him!' shouted the master. The cook's clothes were torn off without delay and he stood trembling between two torturers who had been summoned too. We all started to make excuses on his behalf: 'These things happen, Trimalchio, you can let him off just this once.' Mind you, I for one couldn't understand it. I leaned to a fellow guest and whispered, 'How could any cook worth the name forget to gut a hog? It's criminally careless. If he had served me like that I wouldn't overlook it.' To my surprise Trimalchio let his anger soften. 'So let's have him prove himself as a cook and gut it here.' The cook put on his tunic, grabbed a carving knife and, with a shaking hand, cut open the hog's belly. Suddenly a great stream of sausages, meat-puddings and sweetmeats tumbled out from within. The whole household burst into unanimous applause at this trick that had been played on us: 'Three cheers for the cook!' we all shouted, and the man was rewarded with a glass of wine from a cup made of Corinthian bronze.

Harmless fun, I suppose, but hardly the dinner of a gentleman. If you are too poor to be able to afford a villa suitable for receiving guests, you should consider joining a club. While ostensibly these clubs are designed for you to save for a proper funeral, most hold regular dinners for their members and they are popular among the more respectable lower classes. I act as honorary president for one of these associations. It costs one hundred sesterces to join plus an amphora of good wine. The monthly subscription is one sesterce. On your death your family will receive three hundred sesterces for funeral expenses and fifty for the funeral procession. We hold a dinner every month or so, to which members are obliged to donate an amphora of decent wine, bread and sardines. We have a number of club rules to ensure that these dinners do not degenerate into rowdy affairs. If any member moves about from one seat to another simply to cause disruption, the fine is four sesterces. If any member becomes abusive or obstreperous, the fine is twelve. If anyone is insolent towards me, the president, he is fined twenty. I have to confess that I do not always attend, sending a representative instead, but when I do, I am obliged to wear my toga and make offerings of wine and incense on the birthday of the club's patron goddess, Diana. I also provide members with oil to use in the public baths before they dine.

The higher you rise in society the busier you will become. I am constantly being invited to dinners and functions. Yesterday, for example, I attended the ceremony to celebrate a friend's son's assumption of the manly toga; then a lunch to celebrate a wedding; another friend asked me to attend a hearing in court that concerned him; another wanted me to be a witness to his will; and yet another wanted me to help support him in gaining a political post. How many days have I spent on such trifles in Rome? But if I can escape to the country it is all so different. There I can concentrate on my studies or on looking after myself in gentle exercise or in the baths. I don't have to listen to endless gossip or tell my clients what to do. I live undisturbed, conversing only with my books. This is the noblest of all work. Happy is the man who refrains from business and cultivates his family estates, who doesn't lend money or fight in the army and avoids the business of the forum. Instead, he trains his vines and watches his cattle as they graze, or lies beneath an ancient oak on the matted grass listening to the birds warbling in the trees.

·· COMMENTARY ··

Wealthy, high-status Romans had a pretty snobbish attitude to those who had to work for a living. Cicero lists various occupations that he considers to be unacceptably vulgar for the gentleman to pursue (*On Duties* 1.42 and 2.87–9). Ordinary Romans, though, could not afford to be so choosy. It is easy for us to lump all these non-elite Romans together but their society was as highly graded and differentiated as that at the top. Learning a trade was fundamental to improving quality of life, with skilled labour earning in the region of double the rate of unskilled labour. Manual labour itself came in many kinds: agricultural work in the countryside, building and portering in the cities. Just because the Romans had a lot of slaves did not mean they were spared from working for a living. Falx's final eulogy for the joys of farming bears very little resemblance to the life of back-breaking toil which most peasants faced and it can be found in Horace's second *Epode*.

Work for the wealthiest consisted of the duties imposed by a life of leisure: taking part in public affairs, acting as patron to clients, attending ceremonies and pursuing one's own intellectual interests. Pliny's *Letters* (1.9) give a good example of the kind of general business the wealthy gentleman filled his day doing. It was a common complaint of people like him that he yearned for the peace and quiet of his country estates.

The most respectable form of income was that derived from such estates. Anyone who made some money would soon look to establish themselves in more polite society by investing in such property. Trade was one way in which some social mobility could be attained. Roman wares, from high-quality glass to their beloved fish sauce called garum, were traded right across the empire and beyond. The upper classes looked down on such activities but that does not mean they took no part in them. Often they would employ a front man, perhaps one of their former slaves, to represent them in such business transactions and so prevent them from getting their hands dirty. The elite also invested a lot of money in urban property, even if most did so on a far smaller scale than the legendary Crassus. The jerry-built nature of most urban housing meant that collapse and fire were commonplace. The stories of collapsing property are based on those of Aulus Gellius (*Attic Nights* 15.1) and Cicero (*Letters to Atticus* 14.9). What is particularly striking about Gellius's account of watching a fire break out is that he has no interest in the human element of the event. He neither mentions whether the inhabitants had escaped nor even wonders whether they had done so. His only reaction was to think about the financial risks represented by such investments.

The shape and manner of wearing a toga is actually far from clear. Quintilian's account (*Institutes of Oratory* 11.3) serves to underline how complicated a garment it was. In many ways it was its very uselessness as an item of clothing that made it so valuable as a marker of social status. The fold made at the front of the chest was known as the *sinus* and to become intimate with someone was therefore to insinuate yourself with him. Keeping it clean was a problem, especially as the Romans did not use soap to wash clothes. Instead they used various alkalis, of which urine was the most common. The toga's complexity also meant that it eventually fell out of use for all but certain formal events, such as attending games at which the emperor was present, being largely replaced by the cloak known as a lacerna during the early empire.

The description of Alexandria, attributed to the emperor Hadrian but actually dating much later, can be found in the *Lives of the Later Caesars: Firmus, Saturninus, Proculus and Bonosus* 8. Diocletian's *Edict of Maximum*

Prices, issued in AD 301, lists rates of daily pay for all kinds of artisans and labourers. These prices are given in denarii because there had been a period of high inflation in the third century, so care needs to be taken when comparing them with prices in sesterces from the early empire. The life of the mega-rich Crassus can be found in Plutarch's *Crassus*. The lifetime statistics for the famous charioteer Diocles are from the inscription *CIL* 14.2884. Ammianus Marcellinus has a description of magic being used in the Circus to try to affect the outcome (*Histories* 26.3.3). Caligula's affection for his horse Incitatus is in Dio Cassius *History of Rome* 59.14 and Suetonius *Caligula* 55. The fictitious Trimalchio's over-the-top dinner party is described in Petronius's novel, the *Satyricon*, while details of a more mundane dining-cum-burial club are best seen in the inscription *CIL* 14.2112.

' CHAPTER IV '

ROMANCE LIKE A ROMAN

I F WE COULD LIVE WITHOUT wives we would
spare ourselves a great deal of annoyance. But nature
has ordained that we cannot live easily with or without
them and since we must have them we should think
hard about what form our involvement with them
should take. Above all, you should remember that it is
best to think long-term and put future well-being ahead
of short-term pleasure.

Selecting a wife is a difficult task and here I shall show
you what to look for in an ideal woman. Do not be put
off by my frank admittance that living with a wife is hard.
Some of my friends, out of loyalty to their wives, say
their marriages are not full of annoyances and that such
arguments as do arise are small and easily forgotten. Or
they say that such squabbles are not the inevitable result
of getting married but the fault of individual husbands
or wives behaving badly towards each other. But any
husband knows the truth of what I say. I speak sincerely,
not because I love my wife less than they do, but because

I do not want to make false promises to bachelors among you who are wavering about whether to take the plunge and get married. Rather I wish to dissuade and deter those who have an unrealistic view of what married life entails.

When it comes to selecting a woman the first thing to consider is what you need her for. The first reason is, of course, the need to procreate. The simple fact is that Rome cannot survive without numerous marriages. Without sons to fight in the legions, and girls to marry them, the state would soon wither. My wish is to ensure that those who plan to take on such a great responsibility do so in the full awareness of its importance and a frame of mind that is determined to make it work.

Think hard about the possible candidates. If you look only for beauty in a wife she will think she has fulfilled your wishes without delivering in any other area. She will not mind if she is careless in the home and lets it go to pot. And you will feel obliged to accept this because you married her only on account of her beauty and so had not expected her to be able to do anything practical. The same is true when it comes to marrying a wife who is of high rank or rich. You should not, therefore, take only the girl's family background into account. Wealth, high birth and beauty play no part in a happy marriage. They do nothing to generate interest or sympathetic thought in a wife towards her husband, indeed the very opposite could be said to be the case. Nor do they help when it comes to producing children. You should check to see that her family has a good track record in producing healthy, male heirs. When it comes to a girl's physique, all that matters is that she is healthy, looks normal and has a capacity for hard work. If she is less than beautiful she will be less exposed to efforts by other men to tempt her into adultery, and if she has a strong body she will be better suited to physical labour and bearing children.

You should look for a girl whose character exhibits self-control and virtue. Of course, these are qualities that you should look to display yourself in your own conduct. The reality is that if husband and wife do not share the same outlook on life then there is no hope that their marriage can be advantageous to either party. How could two partners who are unkind to each other ever live in harmony? Just as a crooked piece of wood cannot be made straight or two crooked ones be joined together, or even one straight one with one crooked one, a partner who lacks virtue will spoil a marriage all by him- or herself.

If you own estates that are too large for you to manage on your own, it is hugely beneficial to have a partner whom you can trust to look after them competently in your absence. Man has a nature that makes him active, public and independent; women prefer to stay at home and keep out of sight: each complements the other. The woman is happy to let the man manage her assets. When the husband is away, she is able to carry out his instructions to ensure that the estate continues to run smoothly until he returns.

What is my wife like, you ask? Claudia, for that is her name — a name indeed she shares with her two sisters — is beautiful in many men's eyes but to me she seems fair, small and upright. She lacks sensuality in that she stands more like a statue than a human being and is utterly humourless. But she is extremely attractive and has stolen many of the gifts of Venus for herself. She laughs sweetly and when I gaze at her my senses go numb. The man who lies next to her is, to my mind, the equal of a god. She can spin wool swiftly and manages the household slaves firmly. She has borne and raised four children, though only three of them are still alive, as well as a few others who died in infancy or during birth.

You may, reader, be a girl whose father is considering an offer of marriage on your behalf. Firstly, do not be so silly as to resent this. Marriage is not simply an affair of the heart. It involves the joining together of two families, each with their own interests to maintain. You will also need a dowry appropriate to your family's station in society and you cannot be expected to concern yourself with such weighty matters. You would do well to remember that your virginity is not entirely yours: one third belongs to your father, one third to your mother, and one third to yourself. Do not fight against the parents who have invested so much expense in bringing you up and are going to hand over both their beloved daughter and a large sum of money to your future husband.

I once had to seek out a husband for my fourteen-year-old niece, whose father had died some years previously. There could be no more important task in regard to a young girl. Thankfully, my friend Minutius Aemilianus seemed perfect for this purpose. He holds me in as deep affection as I do him and he models himself on me in the same way that I did on my niece's father. At thirty-five, he is in the prime of life and has already served as Tribune of the People and Praetor. His maternal grandmother was Serrana Procula, of Patavium, a town whose citizens are famed for their virtuous character. His uncle, Acilius, is a man of exceptional gravity, wisdom and integrity. In short, there was nothing in their family unworthy of my own. Minutius himself also had plenty of desirable attributes, being vivacious, amiable, hard-working and modest. He has fine, well-bred features and a ruddy complexion, while his manners exude elegance and gracefulness. I might also add that his father is extremely rich. I know it is vulgar to mention money but we cannot ignore completely the spirit of the age in which we live. We are all ranked by and treated according to our wealth and it would be foolish to imagine that knowing how to live with wealth is not an issue. And, indeed, they made a perfect match – he, a successful and caring husband, she a dutiful and yielding wife.

When my father first introduced me to my future wife he gave me some sound advice about dealing with women that I now pass on to you. 'Do not tire of praising her face, her hair, her graceful fingers and delicate feet,' he said. 'Telling her she's beautiful pleases even the most chaste girl because for virgins their beauty is a source of both pleasure and fear.' How right he was. You should make sure that your fiancée enters the relationship with a positive frame of mind. Too little attention at this early stage can easily leave her sour and uncooperative. Bring in the gods by way of comparison and avoid talking about her faults. If she is emaciated tell her she is slender, if bloated then call her fulsome. Don't ask her age, especially if her flower is already wilting and she is having to pluck out grey hairs from her head.

If none of this wins her over you could try magic. When a friend of mine was once pursuing a girl without success, he was advised of the following love spell by an Egyptian magician: 'Aphrodite's Name, which becomes known to nobody quickly, is NEPHERIE'RI – this is the name. If you wish to win a Woman who is beautiful, do not have sex for three days, then make an offering of Frankincense, and call this name over it. Approach the woman you love and say it seven times in your head as you gaze at her, and in this way it will succeed. Do this for seven days.' I have to say that I think he ended up alarming the girl by staring at her while muttering away under his breath. In any case it certainly didn't work. But I have also heard it said that writing the girl's name in donkey blood on a strip of papyrus then moistening it with vinegar and sticking it to the roof of the steam room at the baths works wonders.

Girls wishing to win over their men should take special care regarding their facial appearance. A radiant complexion will overcome all but the most obvious lacks in looks. I can recommend to female readers the following treatment that my mother swore by to keep the face fresh and bright, even first thing in the morning. First strip away the husks from two pounds of barley, preferably the variety that is imported from Libya. Moisten an equal amount of vetch with ten eggs. Leave the barley to dry in the wind, then crush it with a rough millstone turned by a lazy donkey. Grind up, along with the barley, the horns of a lusty young stag. Add twelve narcissus bulbs, which have been stripped of their outer layers and pulverised on a pure marble counter. Finally, add nine times as much honey. Cover your face with this mixture overnight and your skin will be smoother and shinier than your own mirror.

Or if you suffer from spots, try the following: take six pounds of baked lupins and beans and grind them together. Add white lead and iris, which has been kneaded by strong and sturdy arms. Add some honey from Attica to bind the mixture together. A mixture of incense and nitre is good for blackheads. Take four ounces of each and add some gum from the bark of a tree and a little oily myrrh. Crush the whole lot together and pass through a sieve. Again, bind the mixture with honey. Some women recommend adding fennel as well. Finally, sprinkle with dried rose petals and pour on barley water. Apply the lotion to the skin and you will soon have a charming complexion.

Be careful if you plan to dye your hair. A woman I once knew was always messing around with the colour of her hair. It made her hair fall out. Her wonderful locks, which used to hang down to her waist like fine silk, all lay on the ground. She was even lucky enough to have a natural curl that meant she never had to bother with hot curling irons. Her slave-in-waiting had the easiest job looking after her mistress's hair. She never had to use pins or combs or battle with tangled knots. Her mistress never had to grab a pin and stab the slave girl in the arm to make her stop pulling with her brush. But once her hair was all gone she had to buy herself a blonde wig made from the hair of captured German tribeswomen. It wasn't the same.

Women should also pay special attention to their breath and other personal odours. There is nothing more likely to repulse the advances of an amorous man than the waft of a foul stench. There is a good joke about a young actor who was loved by two women, one of whom had roaring halitosis, while the other was cursed with reeking armpits. 'Give me a kiss,' said the first woman. 'Give me a hug,' whispered the second. But he just cried, 'Alas, what shall I do? I am stuck between a pair of evils!'

If you find a suitable match, you must decide what kind of marriage to have. The traditional type is to admit the woman into your house as a member of your family. Your wife then loses her rights of inheritance from her former family and becomes subject to your authority. But almost everyone these days opts for the more modern, relaxed kind. In this free marriage, your wife remains a member of her original family and remains under the authority of her father. The great advantage of this arrangement is that it is easily annulled if the match turns out to be unhappy or unproductive, but more of that later.

Make sure that you choose an auspicious day for the wedding to prevent ill omens from cursing the marriage at the outset. You would not, for example, wish to hold the ceremony on the third day before the nones of August, that terrible date when Hannibal inflicted such a crushing defeat on us Romans at Cannae. The last days of June are usually a particularly pleasing period. For the wedding itself, the bride wears a red veil and a simple white dress bound by the Herculean knot that the husband must later untie. The ceremony starts with a sacrifice and the reading of the auspices. Next a marriage contract is signed before witnesses and an image of the father of the state, the emperor. A woman who has only been married once then places the couple's right hands together and a silent exchange of vows takes place between them. Then it is time for the fun to start at a fine wedding feast.

At the end of the banquet, the groom pulls the bride from her mother's arms while she pretends to resist. This is done in memory of the rape of the Sabine women, without which Rome itself would not have survived. A procession then takes the bride to the groom's home during which the other people in the group make obscene jokes about what the groom is going to do to her once he has her in his bed. He waits for her inside the house. Once she has arrived, he lifts her over the threshold, making sure that her feet do not touch the ground. Once he has done so, she is part of his family. The couple then perform brief prayers to the household gods and all is done. The guests depart and the couple are left to themselves.

It is only natural that many girls are nervous at this point. I heard of one who fled screaming from the house because she was so worried about the loss of her virginity. I remember my own wedding night. My wife was a young girl of fourteen, while I was close to thirty. She was trembling in fear when I got into bed and removed her dress. Wishing to show her my generous side, like many men on their wedding night I penetrated her through the anus as if she were a boy. Only on the second night did I couple with her in the more usual way and deflower her.

Some husbands can find their new wives resistant to their advances, whether out of anxiety or dissatisfaction with their new partner. If she refuses to be kissed, kiss her all the same. She may struggle at first and shout at you to leave her alone. But if she does fight it will be a losing battle. Mind you, you should be careful not to be too rough with her or kiss her too hard and hurt her mouth. Don't make her hate you on the first night. Going to the next stage may also require you to act forcefully. Do not worry about this. Women like being hurt. What they like to give, they love to be robbed of. Every woman taken by force in a storm of passion is transported with delight. Nothing could be more pleasurable to her. But when she comes forth unscathed from a tussle in which she might have been taken by assault, however pleased she may try to look, she is sorry in her heart. After all, Phoebe and her sister Hilaira were raped but that didn't stop them loving their ravishers in the slightest.

I have to admit I now blush to proceed. But Venus urges me to cover what is, after all, the most important part of the whole matter. Women should enter the fray of love's bedtime battles in the position best suited to their charms. If you have a beautiful face, you should lie on your back so that your husband can enjoy gazing upon the details of your features. If you think that your legs are your most attractive aspect, you should make sure that you show them off by placing your legs on his shoulders. If you are short, let your lover play the part of the rider but, if you are tall, you should kneel in front of him with your head turned slightly to the side. If your thighs still have the firmness of youth or your breasts are flawless then lie across the bed and let your hair fall loose about your shoulders. If the labours of Lucina, the goddess of childbirth, have taken their toll, you should turn your back on the struggle. I could go on. Love can adopt a thousand positions. The easiest and least tiring one is simply to lie on your right side.

Male readers might well be worried about whether they will be able to last out the battle, as it were. Stamina in bed is something that comes with practice and training like anything else. But I am also able to offer you a special potion that I came across while travelling in Egypt from a local man who was well versed in all the black arts and had a spell for every occasion:

Spell to Make You Able to Copulate a Lot:
Grind up fifty small pine cones with a cup of sweet wine and two peppercorns, then drink it.

I remember that one woman I slept with demanded I perform nine times in one short night and it was too much even for me. Thankfully, I had another potion to hand that I can share with you. So if you are having trouble maintaining an erection, try the following recipe: 'Grind up pepper with some honey and mix in nettle and nasturtium juice then smear it over your genitals.' It works every time. Alternatively, you could make use of the pornographic booklets of Musaeus or Sabellus to arouse yourself.

Marriage may be about bearing children – indeed, a marriage is not legally consummated until a child has been produced – but we naturally do not always want sexual congress with our partners to result in pregnancy. Even within marriage, some women are so fertile that they need to have some respite from being pregnant. I can, I am happy to say, recommend a variety of methods of contraception. You must be careful to avoid intercourse at those times that are favourable to pregnancy. It also helps if you smear the entrance to the uterus with old olive oil or honey or sap from a cedar or balsam tree, either on its own or mixed with some white lead. You could also add a clump of fine-spun wool. All of these things have a clogging and cooling effect and cause the entrance of the uterus to close, which does not allow the sperm to pass through. Another traditional method is to make use of a particular type of hairy spider, which has a very large head. If this is cut open, you will find inside two small worms. Take these and tie them to the woman with a strip of deer hide and she will not then get pregnant. I have heard it said that this remains effective for one year.

I also have another spell from my man in Egypt, if you prefer such superstition:

The Best Contraceptive in the World
Take as many seeds of the bitter vetch plant for the number of years you wish to remain sterile. Soak them in the blood of a menstruating woman. Then take a live frog and throw the bitter vetch seeds into its mouth so that the frog swallows them. Let the frog go free near to where you caught it. Then take a seed of stinking nightshade and soak it in mare's milk. Stir in some barley grains, the nasal

mucus of a cow and earwax from a mule before
putting the whole mixture into a deerskin bag. Tie
the bag with a strip of mule hide and then wear it
as an amulet during the waning of the moon in a
female sign of the zodiac.

It is safer to prevent conception than to destroy the
foetus through abortion. It is often the case that a girl
who destroys the children in her womb dies herself. This
is perhaps only fair in that no lioness dares to destroy
her own cubs. Indeed, the funeral procession of one girl
who had died in this way passed by me the other day and
everyone who saw it shouted out, 'She deserved it!' But
we would be naive to imagine that abortion will never
happen, so if you are to do it make sure you do so in
the manner I describe. In order to dislodge the embryo,
make the woman take strenuous walks and be shaken
up by riding on horseback. She should also jump about
violently and lift objects that are far too heavy for her.
If this doesn't work, place her in a mixture of linseed,
marsh mallow and wormwood, which has been boiled.
She should also apply poultices of the same substance to
her vagina and drink old olive oil mixed with rye, honey
and iris.

Just as it is natural for a wife to be utterly faithful to
her husband, so it is for a husband to seek sexual gratification with others. Time takes its toll on all of us and
it is inevitable that many men will tire of their partner.
It reminds me of the story of when the censor was con-
ducting the formal oath concerning wives as part of
taking the census. The formula was as follows: 'If it please

you, do you have a wife?' One joker couldn't resist reply-
ing, 'Indeed I do have a wife, but by Hercules she doesn't
please me.' I heard a much better joke the other day: an
intellectual was about to die and his wife said, 'If you die,
I shall hang myself.' The intellectual said, 'Why not make
me happy while I'm still alive?'

If you wish to commit adultery with another man's
wife then you should be careful. Adultery is a crime
against the husband and it is legal for him to exact a substantial punishment. If he catches you he might choose
to flog you with rods, hurl you from the roof, force you
to pay a large sum in compensation, urinate over you,
cut off your testicles or violate you with a large radish.
So be warned. But if you insist on taking this path, then
you would do well to listen to my advice on how best
to carry out the affair.

Focus your attention on the theatre. You will find all
kinds of women to your taste there: the kind looking for
a quick dalliance, those who want only a quick grope
and a kiss, and others who want you all for their own.
Like ants that pass by in long rows or bees hovering
round colourful blooms, the theatre is full of crowds of
lovely women, all brightly dressed and chatting. They
come to see and, more importantly, be seen. All their
natural modesty seems to go out of the window. You will
find it hard to make a choice from such a constellation
of stars.

Once you have selected your mistress, the Circus
Maximus is a prime site if you are looking for a place to
meet her safely in public. The packed crowd offers many
advantages. You don't have to pretend not to notice each

other or use a secret sign language as you would at a dinner party where your spouses are present. Here you can sit right next to her and squeeze up beside her as closely as possible. It's very easy because the narrow seats force you to do it anyway. Make sure you show great interest in the horses she likes and cheer them on with her. Perhaps a speck of dust will settle on her breast – it often happens with all those horses galloping around the dirt track – so be sure to brush it off with your hand. Even if there isn't any dust, pretend there is and keep brushing off nothing. The Circus provides so many opportunities. If her skirt is trailing along the ground, pick it up for her. She'll thank you for your concern and you'll be able to look at her legs while doing so. Also, turn around to whoever is sitting behind her and ask him not to poke her in the back with his knees. It all shows concern. Many men have found it useful to bring along a cushion to offer their girlfriends. Or you can fan her with the racing programme. It is little touches like these that win over simple female hearts.

Of course, there will come a time when you will want to put a stop to such an attachment. A playful pastime is all well and good but if it lasts for too long eyebrows will be raised and it may even antagonise your wife. If you want to fall out of love, avoid having too much free time and be busy. Cupid's arrows find it easiest to hit their mark when the target is at rest. Keep moving and Venus's mischievous boy will soon lose interest. Look to your business affairs, hang out in the forum, spend time with your friends or join the army. If you cannot find anything useful to do, play dice. Or drink a lot of wine, which desensitises the spirit and keeps love's pangs at bay. Eventually love will give up and leave you alone.

If you cannot be bothered to go through all the hassle associated with having an affair you'll find that prostitutes offer a simple route to sexual gratification. If you think that young men should be forbidden from mixing with prostitutes then you are too harsh and, I might add, against both the spirit of the age and traditional practice. When did young men not act like this and when was it ever forbidden? Young men should frequent brothels in order to gain experience and enjoy some release from their sexual urges, rather than committing adultery with respectable women. It is better to visit a prostitute than gnaw away at the wives of others and lust after any woman who happens to wear a wedding ring on her finger. Indeed, as my dream interpreter, Artemidorus, said to me, dreaming of having sex with a prostitute signifies a little disgrace and a small expense. They are cheap and it does no harm. You can go too far, though. The poet Horace showed no restraint when it came to sex. He kept prostitutes in a mirrored bedchamber positioned in such a way that wherever he looked he saw a reflection of sexual congress.

Prostitutes are easy to find. One of the nicest brothels I ever went to was in the temple of Aphrodite in Corinth. The temple owned more than a thousand female slaves who had been dedicated to the goddess by devout followers. These were available for hire by visitors wishing to honour the goddess by having sex within the precincts. Their fame soon spread and such was their popularity that the city became crowded with tourists and grew rich.

Sadly, the quality of prostitutes in Rome is nowhere near so high. For a long time Greece and Syria have been pouring their human dregs into our great city. Everywhere you go you hear foreign languages and alien customs, and the Circus Maximus is surrounded by the womenfolk of these countries sent out to work the streets. I have had some awful experiences there. One old whore I went with was decked in wigs to cover her baldness, while her face was rutted with wrinkles and looked like that of an aged ape. She had only four teeth left and her breasts sagged like spiders' webs, her voice croaked like a frog and her breath smelled like a piss-pot crossed with the stench of a he-goat fresh from rutting.

It is often simplest to have intercourse with your slaves. They are your possessions to take pleasure from as you see fit. Many masters have a favourite boy whom they dress in women's clothes in order to exaggerate his beauty. Be careful not to keep them like this for too long. Once they approach manhood these boys look ridiculous as they fight a losing battle against their age. Even though he has the physique of a soldier he only remains beardless because he spends hours plucking out his facial hair.

If you have sex with your female slaves be careful not to do so in a way that makes your wife jealous. If you turn your back on her in the marital bed after an afternoon spent canoodling with a young girl in the servants' quarters you are asking for trouble. Of course, you won't bear the brunt of her anger. It will be the poor slave girl who will suffer. The mistress of the house will tear out her hair and have the clothes ripped from her back as she tries to style the mistress's own locks. 'Why is this curl so high?' she will scream and for this heinous crime she will stab her in the hand with a hairpin or have her punished with a whipping.

And on the topic of sex with slaves, I have often observed that this is a common subject of dreams. Indeed, sex of all kinds often occurs in dreams and I should advise you what this signifies. If you dream that you are penetrated by a slave this is not good as it signifies being hated or hurt by the slave. If you are a woman and dream of being penetrated by an acquaintance this is good, especially if he is rich. If a man dreams of handling his own penis he will in real life have sex with his slave, because his hands are serving him in the same way that a slave does. Concerning unnatural sex, to dream of having sex with your son when he is under the age of five is bad news because it means they will die. If the son is between five and ten years of age, he will be sick and the dreamer will lose money in a business affair since it is stupid to have sex with a child at that age. But if the boy is an adolescent then it is good as it signifies a transfer of substance and property to him at the proper age. If you dream of performing oral sex on someone who is an acquaintance, whether man or woman, then you will become enemies as it is no longer possible to share mouths together in conversation. Some dreams are hard to interpret. One man dreamt that his penis was covered with hair and that a thick shaggy fur started to grow on it all the way up to the farthest point of the tip. The man was a notorious passive homosexual who indulged in every form of sexual pleasure, except that he did not use his penis as men usually do. For this reason this part of his body was so inactive that even hairs grew on it, for it was not rubbed against any other body.

There are always some who wish to indulge in strange sexual practices. Some men enjoy taking the passive role. Others go so far as to actively adopt female fashions. They twist their hair in ringlets and soften their whole body with various cosmetics or they pull out their body hair and wear clothes in the likeness of women. They even move like them by walking softly on their tiptoes. This kind of behaviour does not arise naturally in human beings. Nor does anyone believe that effeminate or sexually passive men are suffering from a disease. It is when modesty has been suppressed and lust given free rein that such activities begin. Once men like this are dressing like women it is a sure sign, not that they have any physical affliction, but that they have corrupted minds. Similarly, those women who get sexual gratification from rubbing against other women, and often do so with even greater lust than any man would, have an affliction of the mind. Some doctors believe that effeminate or sexually passive men were created when they were conceived because the male and female seed failed to mix properly in the womb. It is comparable to the way that excessive movement from the woman during intercourse often results in a child with an unstable mind. Other doctors say the fault is inherited and blame humanity for being unable to cleanse itself of such a dysfunction. Whatever its cause, I cannot deny that such practices are common and easily found if you wish to discover them. In fact, you will even find them alluded to in scrawls on walls: 'Felix sucks dick for peanuts' was one I saw on my front wall recently.

You may ask whether sex is preferable with women or young men. Here are some of the arguments people put forward in favour of both. First, many say that sex gives greater pleasure if it lasts longer. Swift delights are gone before we realise they have come upon us. In this regard, many say that the services rendered by a woman are far superior to those of a boy. From maiden to middle age, and even when the crow's feet of old age have trampled over her face, a woman is always a pleasant armful for a man to hug. And however old and however long gone is the beauty of her past, how skilled and experienced she is in the ways of pleasing a man. By contrast, they say that if a man makes attempts on a boy of twenty it seems to be unnaturally lustful, the pursuit of a love between equals that can never be. By then, the limbs are hard, manly and covered with hairs, while chins that were once soft are rough with bristles. As for the parts below … But whatever a woman's age, her hairless skin gives radiance to all parts of her body and her luxuriant ringlets of hair, cascading down her back and curlier than the celery in the meadow, give bloom to her dusky beauty.

Men's intercourse with women involves shared enjoyment. But no one could be so mad as to say that this is the case with boys. The active lover leaves having enjoyed an exquisite pleasure but the one on the receiving end suffers pain and tears, though this does relent with time. And in any case a woman may also be used like a boy and open up two paths to pleasure, so some argue there is no point in having sex with other males. They also say that if men are going to be allowed to sleep with other men then we might as well let women do the same. Let a woman strap on a cunningly contrived sex instrument, that mysterious monstrosity empty of any seed, and lie with another woman as if she were a man. How much better, they argue, that a woman should act like a man than the nobility of the male sex should become effeminate and play the part of a woman!

But others say the opposite. They say that the love of men is the only activity that combines both pleasure and virtue. While marriage is necessary to ensure humanity's continuation, only love for other men can ever be a noble and philosophic union. It is something driven by beauty not by need and is all the more superior for being so. Sex with women was fine when humankind was mired in the daily struggle for existence and the need to reproduce itself, but now that each succeeding generation has become ever more free from such harsh realities so they have had the leisure to devote themselves to higher pursuits. This is how all art has formed. Just as men used to scratch for roots and acorns to eat but now feast on delicacies, so too our advanced form of life means we can indulge in far more pleasurable intercourse than that with women. I shall leave you to decide which path seems best.

When it comes to enjoying yourself sexually, I regretfully have to admit that you can have no worse examples than our emperors. Indeed, their shameful behaviour should warn you of the dangers that unrestrained lust can bring. Caligula had a notorious love affair with the prostitute Pyrallis, and even committed incest with his sisters but, in truth, there was hardly any lady of distinction whom he didn't use as he saw fit. He often invited them and their husbands to dinner and while they lay on their couches would examine the women closely, as if they were slaves. He would then leave the room and summon the one he liked best to be sent to his bedroom. The pair would soon return with their hair and clothes dishevelled and he would comment freely on the woman's sexual performance.

Nero also features high in any sexual hall of infamy. Besides abusing freeborn boys and seducing married women, it is said that he went so far as to debauch the Vestal Virgin Rubria. He castrated the boy Sporus and actually tried to make a woman of him by marrying him with all the usual ceremonies. As someone joked, it was a shame for the world's sake that Nero's own father didn't have a wife like that. Decked out in the finery of an empress, Sporus accompanied Nero in a litter as he travelled through Rome and the emperor would fondly kiss him from time to time. Nero yearned to have sex with his own mother, Agrippina, and it is said that he did so whenever he shared a litter with her, which you could tell from the stains on his clothing. His wantonness was so great that he even devised a new kind of sex game in which he would dress up in a wild animal skin, be let loose from a cage, and then attack the genitals of both men and women who had been tied to wooden stakes. I have heard it said that Nero's firm conviction was that all men were impure and, however chaste they appeared, in reality just concealed their sexual vices. He therefore pardoned all other crimes if the accused confessed to him what those hidden vices were.

If the winner's crown of the imperial sexual Olympics had to be awarded, however, it would undoubtedly go to Tiberius. In his retreat on the island of Capri, they say that he created a suite specially designed for lewdness. Its walls were covered with salacious paintings and many lascivious sculptures were on display. On its many beds, the emperor entertained groups of girls and young men who had been carefully selected for their expertise in sexual deviance. If his own lust was flagging he would have them copulate before him in threesomes. The suite even contained an erotic library so that any participant could find an illustration of what was required of them.

But his predilection for depravity grew even grosser. He allegedly trained little boys, whom he called tiddlers, to crawl between his thighs while he was swimming and tease him with their licks and nibbles. He even used young babies to perform fellatio on him, as if they were feeding at the breast. The story is also told that at one particular sacrifice he was so overcome with lust for a young participant in the ceremony that he lost control of himself and rushed him off to his bedroom where he debauched both the boy and his brother, who was one of the flute players. When they subsequently complained about the assault, he had their legs broken.

I suspect that there are some tall tales here. But even more modest emperors, like Augustus, knew how to have fun. Augustus enjoyed adultery although he often claimed to partake in it as a matter of policy, because it allowed him to find out from wives what their husbands were really thinking. His friends used to supply him with well-born women and girls, who they would personally strip and inspect to ensure their suitability. He treated marriage as a political matter. As a young man, he was engaged to the daughter of Publius Servilius Isauricus, but when he became reconciled with Mark Antony after their first falling out, the armies of both men insisted on a family alliance to cement the relationship. He therefore married Antony's stepdaughter, Claudia, although at that time she was scarcely of marriageable age. But when he had an argument with his mother-in-law, Fulvia, he divorced her untouched, and left her a pure virgin. Soon afterwards he married Scribonia, who had been married twice to men of consular rank, and had a child by one of them. When she complained about his dalliances, Augustus simply divorced her, saying that he was quite exhausted by the perverseness of her temper. Immediately he married Livia Drusilla, even though she was already pregnant by her husband Tiberius, and from that time on she never had any rival in his love and affection.

Despite these acts, Augustus was keen to improve the public morals of Rome. He passed laws to control adultery and to punish those who are caught committing acts of debauchery, violating the marriages of others or seducing virgins or respectable widows. Fathers were permitted to kill their daughters and partners in adultery. Husbands were required to divorce adulterous wives. Offenders could also be exiled to an island, so long as it was a different island from their lover. Augustus himself had to prosecute his own daughter, Julia, whose lecherous behaviour was the talk of Rome, and he exiled her to the island of Pandateria in the Tyrrhenian Sea. He also wished to encourage marriage and the bearing of legitimate children. Fathers were rewarded for having children, particularly if they had three boys, while those of marriageable age who refused to get married were debarred from receiving inheritances and from attending the public games. It all goes to show: you should do as emperors say and not as they do.

·· COMMENTARY ··

Rome was a patriarchal society that saw women of all ages as requiring male guidance and protection. Marriages were semi-arranged between two families, with the fathers playing a key role (see Pliny's *Letters* 1.14). Catullus says (*Poem* 62) that a girl's virginity belonged one third to her father, one third to her mother and only one third to herself. A girl's wishes would easily be overridden in a family context where she had been brought up to obey her father's wishes completely. It is not clear at what age most Roman girls got married. Some inscription evidence suggests that sixteen to eighteen years of age was normal although the cost of such inscriptions may mean we are seeing only the view of the wealthier classes who could afford to keep their girls at home for longer. Twelve was the legal minimum age to marry although there are examples of girls marrying younger than this. In any case, this was a world without birth certificates where most people probably only had a fairly vague notion of exactly how old they were. Girls were often married to men significantly older than themselves and we can only imagine how stressful this might have been for them. In one example, a girl runs off from her new husband's house because she is so terrified at what awaits her. It is possible that the practice of anal sex on the first night was common as it is alluded to in a knowing way by both Seneca (*Controversies* 1.2.22) and Martial (*Epigrams* 11.78).

Marriage seems to have been more a matter of business than love. In the *Oracles of Astrampsychus*, of the ten possible answers to the question 'Will I marry and will it be to my advantage', only one says that the petitioner will marry someone he or she knows and wants to marry. A majority of the marriages, the oracle says, will be unhappy relationships, full of regret, and there will be a high divorce rate. The very way the question is phrased to focus on personal gain underlines what was perhaps the usual attitude to marriage. That is not to say that Roman marriages were never based on love or that deep bonds of affection never developed between the two partners. But it is clear that marriage was seen as a duty and a burden, which is reflected in the discussion to be found in Gellius *Attic Nights* (1.6) and Musonius Rufus (*Discourses* 13b).

Ovid is our best source for many aspects of Roman attitudes to sex, although it is impossible to say how representative these were of more ordinary people. The view that women like it rough can be found in his *Art of Love* (1.663–80). Various beauty treatments can be found in his *On the Facial Treatments of Ladies*. Ovid offers a cure for impotence in *Loves* 3, as does Petronius *Satyricon* 138, while the *Greek Magical Papyri* contain the equivalent of ancient Viagra (7.184–5). Ovid also wrote a *Cure for Love*, which tells you how to fall out of love. We have various references to the use of pornographic booklets for masturbation or titillation but none survive (e.g. Martial 12.95; 12.43). The medical writer Soranus, who sounds like a doctor in a *Carry On* film, contains much information about the supposed nature of women, contraception and matters relating to pregnancy and childbirth (see his translation into Latin by Caelius Aurelianus). On the use of radishes to punish adulterers, see Horace *Satire* 1.2 and Catullus *Poem* 15.

Male attitudes towards the use of prostitutes seem to have been very relaxed, and even temples, such as the one at Corinth, would sometimes act as brothels (Strabo *Geography* 8.6.20). The astrologer Firmicus Maternus (*Eight Books of Astrology* 3.5.23; 3.6.15) and Seneca both talk of men cross-dressing and adopting female postures (*Moral Letters* 122.7). The work, *The Two Kinds of Love*, ascribed to Lucian, discusses the pluses and minuses of sex with women and boys. The Romans do not seem to have been overly bothered who their men had sex with so long as they were the active partner. Suetonius's *Lives of the Caesars* is the best place to find racy gossip about the intimate lives of various emperors but it should be taken with more than a pinch of salt. In reality, most people did not enjoy the sexual freedoms that their imperial masters did and Augustus tried to impose higher standards of personal behaviour, however impossible this must have been to enforce widely. Sadly, one high-profile victim of Augustus's moral clampdown was the poet Ovid, whose witty verses about matters sexual and adulterous clashed with the official line (he may also have had an affair with a Vestal Virgin). This sophisticated Roman urbanite was consequently exiled to Tomis on the Black Sea, the deadest backwater Augustus could think of, and poor Ovid was left there to rot until his death.

· CHAPTER V ·

HOW TO MANAGE
YOUR FAMILY

WHAT MAKES A GOOD WIFE? How should
children be brought up? These are vital questions to answer if you are to benefit from the joy that
a well-managed household can bring. What man could
ever be happy while his wife conducts barely concealed
love affairs with multiple partners or his children openly
disobey him? Let me explain how to ensure the efficient
and orderly running of your family.

I shall begin by describing my own wife's virtues.
Marriages as long as ours are rare – we are lucky enough
to have been married for over twenty years – and it has
taught me what makes a good wife. To begin with, she
is incomparably discerning and thrifty. Her devotion to
me radiates from her face and advertises her faithfulness
for all to see. It has also driven her to take up reading
so that she can enjoy my own writings, some of which
she has even learned by heart. The harmony between us
grows by the day. Whenever I start out on some project
she is full of concern and when I have finished she is

happier than anyone. If I am speaking in the senate she will send a messenger to report back to her how my speech has been received. When I give public readings from my books, she always sits near to me, hidden behind a curtain, so that she can hear every bit of praise I receive. Love is her guide in all she does. She is not in love with my youth or my looks, which time is steadily eroding. She is in love with my glory. All this she learned from her father, who made sure that she was surrounded from birth only by things pious and moral.

Her domestic virtues know no bounds. She is loyal, obedient, affable and reasonable, and works hard at her wool-making. She is religious without being superstitious, dresses modestly and uses little make-up. She is devoted to her family and has shown as much attention to my own mother as she does to her own. Her generosity has been shown to many friends and loved ones. Only her sister has been her equal in this regard. My wife brought up her younger female relations in our house and made sure that they had sufficient dowries so they could obtain marriages worthy of the family name. I do not mention this to praise myself for donating to the cost of these dowries for members of my wife's family, but purely to make it clear that it was all my wife's idea.

For some years, she despaired of her ability to have children and fell into deep grief about my lacking an heir. She proposed divorce and offered to vacate the house so that another more fertile woman could replace her. She offered to search out another wife whom she felt was worthy of the honour and would prove a suitable match. She even stated that she would not take back her substantial dowry but would devote herself to acting as a kind of sister and mother-in-law to the new wife and would treat any children as if they were her own. Thankfully, at this moment of crisis, she finally fell pregnant and so saved me from making what would have been a difficult decision.

My wife is an impossibly high target for most women to aim at. But for any wives reading this, here are some rules, the fruits of my marital wisdom, which will enable you to ensure that your own husbands are kept happy:

- Do not imagine that the fires of the newly-weds can be kept burning for long. What starts out being driven by lust can only be sustained if a more durable fuel can be found.

- When he takes a woman as a wife, the husband should understand why he has married her. Yes, he wanted her to have children. No, he did not want her to stop looking after him.

- The moon is radiant when far from the sun but disappears when it is close to it. A modest wife should be the opposite: she should be seen in public mostly with her husband, but when he is away on business she should stay at home.

- Just as there is little use in a jewel-encrusted mirror unless it reflects a true likeness, so there is no advantage in a rich wife if she does not conform to her husband's habits. A wife should have no emotion of her own but should reflect the mood of the husband, laugh at his jokes when he is happy and be sad when he is sorrowful.

- A wife should have no friends of her own but should cultivate those of her husband. Nor should she worship any private gods. Her door must be shut to all forms of superfluous superstition and admit only the gods of her husband.

- A happy marriage is one where the words 'mine' and 'yours' are seldom heard. All things, whether good or bad, should be shared, and the bond will be strengthened all the more by it. Nature itself teaches this in the way that it is impossible to tell which part of a child belongs to either parent. So put all your assets together and let the husband manage them on your behalf. For just as we still call watered-down wine 'wine', even if it contains mostly water, so we say that the house and assets belong to the husband even if most of it came into the marriage with the wife.

- A Roman was once criticised by his friends for divorcing his chaste, beautiful and wealthy wife. In response, he took off his shoe and said, 'This is a fine shoe but you don't know where it is pinching me.' In the same way, a wife should not rely on the large dowry she has brought into the marriage to keep him happy. Instead, she needs to be companionable, cheerful and agreeable. It is the routine tiffs – unseen by the wider world – that set a couple at loggerheads and do the greatest injury.

- A woman should never desire to rule her husband. It is the man's lot to govern his wife, not as a master does his slave, but as the soul does the body by sympathy and goodwill.

- Greek generals used to order their men to receive enemy units silently if they ran up shouting, but if they advanced in silence to charge out shouting and screaming. So too a sensible wife will stay quiet during her husband's tantrums but do her best to raise his spirits if he is sullen and moody.

- A wife should, like a bee, gather honey from the knowledge her husband surrounds her with. If he makes it clear that extravagance shall have no place in his side of the house, then nor will gold cups, pictures, decorations for mules or other vanities be seen in her half. It never hurts to hear the wife say, 'Husband, you are my teacher and guide.' And if the husband instructs her in geometry then she will be too ashamed to do silly things like dancing, if he teaches her philosophy she will laugh at those who believe witches can draw the moon down from the sky, and if he helps her understand astronomy she will no longer be terrified by every passing eclipse.

If there is one golden rule, it is that wives should be submissive. As my dream interpreter, Artemidorus, says, 'If a man dreams that he has sexual intercourse with his wife and that she yields willingly, submissively, and without reluctance to the union then it is good for all alike.' A wife should serve her husband as if he were her master, even though he should, of course, treat her better than he does his slaves.

It is terrible to see a husband who has lost a good

wife. Recently, our friend Macrinus was pierced with the severest affliction because his wife died, a woman whose virtues would have stood out even in the distant past. He lived with her for thirty-nine years in the most uninterrupted harmony. How respectful was her behaviour towards him. How she united in her character all the good things of the female life. The only consolation poor Macrinus has is that he enjoyed such a marriage for so long. She was a woman of such generosity and patience that even when she knew her husband was having sex with one of the young slave girls she pretended not to notice. She didn't think it was right for a woman to make accusations against her keeper or for the simple impatience of a wife to be directed at so great a man. She never bore any ill will towards the girl herself and even went so far as to free her and give her to one of her freedmen as a wife.

What wives must do is to give their husbands sons. You should understand how to get pregnant. Just as there are seasons that are better for sowing seed on the ground, so too the seed ejaculated in intercourse will not always bear fruit. In order to achieve the right result, you must be careful to have intercourse when menstruation is ending, when there is an urge to engage in sexual intercourse, and when your body is neither too hungry nor full from excessive eating or drinking. If you are hungry, it is best to have a light snack first.

If pregnancy does occur, be aware that miscarriage is always a risk. My wife once did so when we were first married. She was a young girl and didn't even realise that she was pregnant so failed to take the necessary precautions that a pregnant woman should. If the pregnancy persists to the childbirth stage, make sure you acquire the services of a good midwife. She will be knowledgeable and experienced, calm and unruffled in a crisis, and be able to give a clear account of the procedures she is using. She will reassure her patient and be sympathetic. She will always be sober because she never knows when she will be needed. She will be discreet because she will share many secrets. She definitely won't be superstitious and so will not overlook any possible remedy on account of an omen or some other vulgar superstition.

You read such nonsense about childbirth. I came across the funniest book the other day, which claimed to be an account of how people got pregnant on the moon. It said that babies there were not borne by women but men. In fact, it claimed that men marry men there and do not know the word 'woman' at all. Every man is a wife until he is twenty-five years old and then he becomes a husband. Lacking a womb, they bear their unborn children in the calf of the leg. After conception, the calf begins to swell. In due course they cut the leg open and deliver the child but it is always dead. They bring it to life by putting it in the wind with its mouth open. But that is not the only way they produce new human beings. They have men called Tree-buggers who are brought into the world as follows: they cut off a man's right testicle and plant it in the ground. A very large tree of flesh grows from this, which resembles a giant penis, but has branches and leaves and its fruit are the size of melons. When these ripen, they harvest them and the men pop out from these shells. The book said that moon-men also have artificial body parts made of ivory or, if they are poor, wood, and they use them to have sex. What a ridiculous story – believe it all if you will!

Childbirth is not the only way to acquire children. Before my wife managed to become pregnant I did once purchase a child from a woman who no longer had the means to feed the girl and offered her to me. The child seemed healthy and I made sure that the mother signed a contract relinquishing all claims over her in the future unless she reimbursed me all of the costs of raising her. As it happened, my wife did fall pregnant and so I had no need for the girl. I gave her to one of my slave women to raise as her own child, which she did until the girl died of a fever when only eight or nine. It was fortunate that my wife had not grown attached to the child and so was not overly upset at her death.

Naturally, you will not want to keep every infant your wife gives birth to. An infant does not become fully human until the eighth or ninth day when it is named and accepted into the family by the father. Prior to that, it is the father's decision whether to let it live or to terminate it. Children are expensive and, as head of the family, it is your duty to make sure that there are sufficient resources to go round. Three or four children are desirable since you never know when fate will rob you of one or two of them. Those that survive into adulthood can be expected to look after you in your old age and inherit the family name. So if your wife does produce more babies than is required you should instruct her to abandon them at the town dump or by the roadside. Whether the infant is a girl or a boy will probably influence your decision, since it never hurts to have a spare boy or two, whereas girls are a costly expense who will require a dowry in due course. I once had to order my wife to carry out this unhappy duty. The girl was healthy but had been born under such an inauspicious alignment of the stars that there seemed no point in raising such an ill-fated child, particularly as we had two daughters already. Reluctantly I told my wife to remove the infant from the household in case it should bring ill fortune on all of us. How she begged me over and over again to change my mind but I would not be moved. I understood these things so much better than her and my mind was made up. She left the child by the roadside, although she made sure to tie an amulet about its neck to protect it from danger and by which she might recognise it in the future if fate should ever decide to make our paths cross again. I suppose it does no harm. Mind you, I know plenty of women who simply throw the unwanted babies down the nearest well to be rid of them.

Healthy-looking abandoned babies will often be picked up by slave dealers who will rear them using wet nurses before selling them on when they are aged five or so. Those, too, whose own children have died might be looking to replace them; and indeed people who have been unable to produce children may find babies in this way. It has to be said that not all such babies are picked up, however. Many die of the cold or are eaten by stray dogs.

If you are unfortunate enough to be poor and have too many children, you should consider selling them into slavery. You sometimes see such children begging by the side of the road. They work for gangs who mutilate them by dislocating their limbs and cutting out their tongues to make them more pitiable and so more likely to attract gifts. I have sometimes seen my wife grow pensive when she has encountered beggars who are about the same age as the infant we exposed would now be if it survived. I point out to her that we did tie a necklace around the baby's neck so that we would be able to recognise the child if we did ever meet her.

Another way to reduce the size of your family is to get a member of your wider kin group to take any excess children into their house. Or, if you feel that your poverty is only temporary and wish to keep all your children, you should adjust the family's rations. It is vital to feed the menfolk who are the main wage earners and so need to keep up their strength. Women, girls and weaker children can have their food reduced. Or you could feed them items normally fed to animals, such as acorns or vetch. You should also put your children out to work so that they can add to the family's income, rather than simply being a cost. Boys aged seven or eight can be apprenticed out to artisans, who will not only pay them a modest wage but will also instruct them in a valuable trade. Girls can be found work with jewellery makers, washing clothes in fulleries or making patchwork from old clothes.

The father must ensure that those children you decide to keep receive the proper upbringing. If you leave it up to the mother, she will simply cuddle them and try to protect them from the sun because she hopes they will never have to be unhappy, cry or do anything difficult. A father loves in a different way. He will get them up early so that they can start their studies and will not let them lounge around even during the holidays. He is always prepared to extract both sweat and tears from his children.

Obviously, you will not always be able to be there for your children. You will need to employ a nanny to carry on your good work. Make sure that she speaks correctly. It is the nanny that the child first hears and her words will be the first he will try to imitate. You must always make sure that the nanny is of good character. Children are highly impressionable, and just as strong flavours can easily be absorbed by a new pot, so children can quickly be tainted by the vices of their first carers. It is much easier if the boy does not pick up a bad accent or bad habits in the first place.

It is highly desirable to give children a sound education as early as possible. It is hard to give clear guidance about the exact form this should take. You should be careful not to make them angry or to blunt their natural spirit. Freedom nurtures the spirit, repression crushes it. But if freedom is unchecked, the child will grow insolent and bad-tempered. You must try to steer a middle course between these two extremes, using both carrot and stick to keep the child on a steady path. Do not humiliate the child or treat him as if he were a slave. Never make him act submissively and never let whining reap a reward. Only good behaviour should ever be rewarded.

The boy's education must begin when he is young because he will be quicker to do what you tell him.

Also, if you can train him into good habits early then you will not have to force him to abandon bad habits later in life. If the boy has little shame and doesn't care about honour then educating him is difficult. There is no alternative other than employing fear and terror when he does wrong in order to try to correct his ways.

Education must above all teach the child to tell the truth and avoid lies. If the boy tells a lie, he must be told off and beaten if necessary. Telling the truth is the best of virtues, whereas telling lies is the worst error. Telling lies will never lead to prosperity. He must show respect for his parents, his teachers and other educated people. Any child who fails to do this will never be successful. The young must be taught to serve others. This is particularly so with the children of the rich, who have no need to do what they are told. The boy must not cry, yell or beg if the teacher hits him. To do so is a sign of weakness and cowardice and is the kind of behaviour to be expected from a slave. The boy must be made to hate money and be taught to treat it like a poisonous snake, whose venom enters the body and damages it. He should be allowed time to play but this should be relaxing to give him energies for his studies.

The boy should be taught not to rush up at mealtimes and gaze at his food greedily. A way must be found to minimise the importance of food in his eyes. If he continues to show signs of greed you must tell him that greed is a characteristic of pigs and those who act like pigs cannot be distinguished from one. When he is sitting at the table, he must not be allowed to stretch out his hand to grab whatever he wants. He should restrict himself to taking a few things, which he should eat slowly. He should not take big mouthfuls. He should not get his hands, mouth or clothes dirty. He should not lick his fingers. He should not be the last to finish. He should not sit and stare at anyone else at the table, especially if they are guests. Give him plain bread sometimes to get him used to simple fare and teach him self-restraint. This will be a very useful attitude for him to possess in later life, especially if he is poor. So do not let him eat his fill at breakfast and only let him do so in the evening. It is beneficial for both his mind and body for him not to stuff himself first thing in the morning and it will keep him alert for his lessons.

He should have his meal at the end of his lessons when he is already tired. He should not eat too much meat. Meat slows the mind, makes a child fat and prevents him from growing properly. Only let him have a few sweets and a little fruit, or else he will develop a love of luxury and pleasure. Do not let him drink while eating as it expands the food and makes it heavier. Only give him a drink after he has finished eating. Do not let him drink wine until he is on the verge of manhood because it will damage his body and soul. Wine alters the minds of men and makes them stupid, rude, reckless and angry. How much more is it likely to corrupt a boy? He should not mix with ordinary people as he will be exposed to a lot of rude language and ignorance.

He should not be allowed to sleep for pleasure but only as long as he needs. Too much sleep is harmful as it softens the body and deadens the heart. He should be woken up at dawn and taught to go to the toilet immediately so that all the accumulated impurities are quickly removed from the body. There is nothing more conducive to mental agility, energy levels and overall health than this. He must not be allowed to sleep in the day unless he is ill. He should not be given bedding that is too soft because it will make him develop an equal softness. The boy needs toughening up and for his soul to grow strong, for which only a firm bed will do.

It is better for him to be exposed to some cold in winter and heat in summer than none at all. Otherwise he will grow weak and be delicate and feeble. He should do lots of exercise – walking, running, riding – and not be pampered. He should not be dressed in soft or fine clothes, which will only encourage his interest in womanly things and make him interested in having the money to buy them. He should not go out without a cloak. And when he is out he should not hurry too much when he walks since walking quickly is a sign of recklessness and excessive business. He must not be allowed to have long hair or wear rings or other adornments. Instead, he should be made to realise how disgraceful such effeminate behaviour is for a man. He must never show off his possessions to others who do not have them. He should honour his elders and stand up whenever they enter the room.

The boy must be warned about the dangers of sexual intercourse and discouraged from acquiring any knowledge of it until he is married. It will teach him self-control and will also ensure that his reputation remains unsullied. Abstinence from sex will also help him grow strong physically just as it will make his soul virtuous.

A boy should not have friends who are pushy or aggressive. He should not swear but be friendly and enjoy pleasant discussion. Let him love being competitive about his education and be proud of letting no one do better than him in exams. Let him be proud also that he never takes help from anyone else unless he does something in return. You should take pains to make him enjoy winning without hurting his opponent. And when he does win he should be praised but not excessively so as this will only lead to his having too high an opinion of himself. All this is particularly true of only children who are more likely to be indulged and so have their characters spoiled. Such children cannot cope with criticism or failure because they have never been denied anything and their tears have always been wiped away by their anxious mothers.

Some believe that boys should not learn to read and write until they are seven years old. They argue that before then they are too young to concentrate or cope with the pressures of education. But you would do well not to let your son's mind lie fallow. What else will he do with the time except waste it in idle pleasures and become accustomed to doing so? Early training will exercise the memory when it is at its strongest. I'm not suggesting that a boy be given real work to do. You must make sure that he enjoys and loves his studies, so that he develops the right attitude to learning. Make it fun and competitive, so he can enjoy striving against his peers. Praise him and teach him to enjoy doing well – and let him think he is doing well most of the time. Just do not overdo it, so that he comes to think he will only ever be praised.

As soon as the boy has learned to read and write he should be handed over to the teachers of literature. With them he will learn two things: the art of public speaking and how to read the great poets such as Homer and Virgil. This involves learning a whole range of skills, from performance, to interpretation, to composing poetry. But poetry on its own is not enough. The boy should carefully study all kinds of writers, not just for the subject matter but also for the style. He should too be exposed to music to teach him about metre and rhythm, to astronomy so he may learn how the universe is ordered, and philosophy so he may understand the workings of nature. Discussing such topics requires great fluency and a large vocabulary, so you can see that literature and oratory go hand in hand. It will also be the delight of his old age. For books are the sweet companions of our solitude.

Your daughter's education should be entrusted to her mother. The child should be instructed in how to weave wool, sew and manage the household slaves, especially in the kitchen. Teaching her to read will also enable her to engage in conversation at table, although music is a more fitting accomplishment for a girl than literature. If you are poor, you will have to teach your daughter some more practical skills, such as the preparation of food and cooking – perhaps even how to count, subtract and calculate fractions – but the aim is the same: to make her an attractive prospect for a potential husband.

A word of warning about stepmothers. If you remarry after a divorce or the death of your wife, make sure that you keep an eye on how your new wife treats the children you have had with your former partner. It is only natural that a stepmother would never love her stepchildren by inclination or by choice. She will lavish affection on her own children but hate the ones produced by another woman's birth pangs. She will give them less food and pass it to her own children instead. Before you know it, you will find half your children happy and well fed, while the others sit emaciated and covered in bruises.

Your duties as head of the household extend to keeping an eye on your siblings even in adulthood. After my father's death, I had once to write to my younger brother who was still living with my mother because I had heard that he was not treating her with sufficient respect. 'We ought to revere our mother since she has given birth to us and is, in any case, a model of virtuousness. So make sure you look after her,' I warned him, 'and if I hear again that you are talking back to her I shall come and slap you.'

Ah, my mother – what a goddess! How anxious I was when she fell ill recently. She caught a chill when calling on one of the Vestal Virgins. She grew thin and everything seemed to be heading downhill except her spirits. It pained me greatly that so excellent a woman seemed to be about to leave this world, which will never again see her equal. Twice she followed my father into exile and was once even banished herself because she was covering for him. Since the end of such tyrannical times, she has been able to indulge her skills in pleasant and polite conversation and, gods be praised, has regained some strength. She remains as venerable as she is amiable, a model to hold up to our wives, whose bravery and fortitude is so great that even we men can learn from it.

Sadly, such a female role model is needed now more than ever. Women seem to be getting out of control. Some date this phenomenon back to the role Sempronia played in the Catiline conspiracy. She, they say, was the first woman to act with a masculine daring and boldness despite fortune having blessed her with beauty and a good husband. She was clever, witty and had great charm. She had studied Greek and Latin literature, wrote poetry and could play the lyre. She also danced well, perhaps too well for an honest woman. But she was so filled with burning lust that she made more advances to men than they ever did to her. Even before falling in with Catiline and his conspiracy to overthrow the republic, she had often thought nothing of breaking promises and dishonouring credit agreements. She had even been an accessory to murder.

I place the start of the decline much earlier than that. It was when the Oppian law was repealed that the trouble started. You will recall that this law had been passed after the terrible defeat we suffered at the hands of Hannibal at Cannae, when almost fifty thousand Romans perished in a single day. Realising that something had to be done, the law banned women from owning more than half an ounce of gold, from wearing multicoloured clothes, or from riding in a horse-drawn carriage in the city itself. These and other measures served to stiffen Rome's moral backbone and eventually Carthage was indeed defeated.

Yet peace soon brought calls to repeal the law. Women pressed their husbands and even paraded in the streets and crowded the forum urging men to repeal the laws. What sort of behaviour was this, for women to run in public, block the roads and talk to other women's husbands unchaperoned? Our ancestors never permitted women to conduct themselves in such a way. They were kept firmly under the control of their menfolk. Instead, the women were determined to lose all such restraint. 'We want to glitter with gold and purple,' they cried, and 'We want to ride in carriages whenever we want!' No limits to their spending and luxury, is what they meant. If men had then determined to assert their rights as husbands, we would now have far less trouble with women than we do. Instead, they gave way and our collective freedom was trodden under female foot because husbands failed to control their wives at home. And from that time, women felt free to spend as much as they desired because the law ceased to set a limit on their expenditure and because they knew that their husbands were too weak to impose one at home. It was then that they began to see themselves as our equals and soon, no doubt, will think themselves our superiors.

It is not war that is killing us; it is luxury. Empire has brought us great wealth and from that moment all virtue has been lacking. Money and vice have poured in side by side until we are all soaked in effeminate decadence. Now women feel they can criticise you in public or while reclining at table if you make some small factual error. We Romans may rule all mankind, but our women rule us. Their low status used to keep our women chaste, while hard work kept their hands tough and their hearts honest. Now we suffer the sickness of peace. A doctor friend remarked recently that women never used to lose their hair or suffer pains in the feet, whereas now they need to import hair extensions and are afflicted by gout. The female body has been conquered by the same luxury that long ago defeated our men. Now women drink late and drink more than their male drinking companions. They challenge men to wrestling matches and vomit up the contents of their distended bellies. They are always gnawing ice to relieve their indigestion and, even though they were created to feel passion passively, now they are the equal of men in their lust. They invent new kinds of licentious behaviour and take the active role in sex. When they behave worse than men, is it any wonder so many women are bald and gouty!

Nowadays, women lust after the worst sorts – gladiators, charioteers, actors or even some muscle-bound mule-driver in the street. They open the doors of their houses to any man passing and live like prostitutes. The way they walk and dress, how they make eyes at random men, and how they kiss and cuddle openly at dinner parties, it all displays their inner lasciviousness. One woman I came across, called Eppia, the wife of a senator no less, ran off with a gladiator to Egypt. She abandoned her home and left her tearful children. She even left behind her dear beloved actor, Paris! Even though she had been brought up in the greatest luxury, she now thought nothing of the dangers of sea travel. Undaunted by the rough waves of the Adriatic and the swell of the Ionian Sea, she was dead set on escaping with her lover. And all for what? What was this man who had set her on fire and captured her heart? What was it she saw in him that made it worth becoming a gladiator's moll? Was it the barely healed wounds on his arm or the scars on his head caused by the rubbing of his helmet? Was it the hairy wart on his nose or the smelly discharge dripping from his eye? No, it was enough that he was a gladiator. That made him more beautiful than Hyacinth and worth abandoning her husband, sisters and children for. It's his weapon – if you know what I mean – that she's really in love with.

How times have changed. Egnatius Mecenius once beat his wife to death with a club because she had drunk too much wine. And not only did no one bring him to court because of this, but no one even criticised him. All the decent men agreed she had deserved it because she was setting such a bad example. You can rest assured that any woman who drinks indecent quantities of wine is closing the door to all virtues and opening it up to all manner of vices. Of course, many husbands still do their best to control their wives. You see plenty of women bearing the scars of beatings on their disfigured faces. One such woman once complained about such treatment to my mother, who merely replied that she should think of her marriage vows as the tools by which she had been made into a slave and she should not be insolent towards her master.

Such feisty female behaviour has occurred even in my family. I recently visited my brother Quintus in Arcanum. His behaviour towards his wife was calm and gentle and there was no hint of any quarrel. He said to his wife, Pomponia, in the kindest manner, 'Would you mind asking the ladies in to dinner and I shall fetch the men.'

What could be more courteous than that? But she just snapped back, 'Well, I'm just a guest here myself, aren't I?' I didn't really understand what she meant but obviously she feels uneasy about her insecurity since he owns all the assets. Quintus said to me, 'You see, that's what I have to put up with every day!' I know it wasn't much, but it was very irritating. It made what should have been a pleasant lunch into a doleful affair. She wouldn't even recline at table. Quintus sent some dishes to her room but she petulantly refused them. In short, I've never seen such bad-tempered behaviour. He told me that she even refused to sleep with him. As soon as I returned home I wrote to her brother (her father being dead) to point out how badly his sister was behaving towards my brother and to ask him to sort it out.

Sadly, such differences cannot always be resolved. Let me tell you what you need to do should you decide to get divorced. If you want to end the marriage, all you have to do is inform your wife, either verbally, by letter or by sending a slave to announce it to her. Marriage is based on consent between men and women of marriageable age – with the permission of any relevant guardians – and so once consent has gone there is no longer any basis for the marriage to continue. Of course, the reality is never so simple and in truth it normally takes long negotiations between both families before a settlement is reached.

There is no such thing as joint property. The broad principle is that the woman takes back what she brought into the marriage as her dowry. For this reason I always advise new husbands to keep the full value of the dowry separate so they will be able to repay it quickly should divorce become necessary. The courts insist upon full repayment before they will grant a divorce decree and it can be a real problem if you have married a girl from a wealthy family who has brought with her a significant amount of wealth. If you are not careful it will give your wife a real hold over you, so long as she remains faithful at least. However, if the divorce is her fault, you are entitled to take off child-related costs from her dowry in the ratio of one sixth per child up to a maximum of one half. You may also retain between one eighth and one sixth of the value of the dowry as punishment for any moral failings she has displayed, with adultery counting as the worst. Remember that no divorce is valid unless seven male citizens are present to hear the decree. This is particularly important if your wife has been cheating on you because, if you do not get properly divorced, you might find yourself charged with pimping since she is behaving like a prostitute.

Children belong to the father. Many bitter husbands forbid their former wives from seeing their children again. While this is understandable, you should overcome such anger. It does not benefit your children to be deprived of all maternal influence – however wickedly she may have behaved – and it may even turn them against you. Also, if your wife believes that you may act in this vindictive fashion she may decide to limp on in an unhappy marriage when you could both be free to start again. You would be better advised to separate as amicably as possible and come to a private arrangement whereby the young children stay with the mother while those who have entered education reside in your household. Wherever they live, the children will remain your financial responsibility.

Many legal problems arise when marriages end and the woman then claims to be pregnant. Establishing paternity can be very difficult especially if she has been committing adultery. Since any child, if it can be proved to be yours, will be your financial liability and will count among your heirs, you should only accept the child if you are confident it is yours. You should rely on your calendar, so long as you believe your wife was being faithful to you. Your ex-wife has to declare she is pregnant by you within thirty days of the divorce. You have the right to have her inspected to check that she is pregnant. There have been many cases where bitter former wives have tried to palm off an abandoned baby as their husband's legitimate heir. Once you are convinced that she is carrying your child, you also have the right to keep an eye on her to make sure that she acts appropriately during the pregnancy and then that delivery of the infant happens safely.

Any female readers thinking about getting divorced should take into account the following considerations: if the gods have smiled upon you and you have been fertile enough to produce three or more children, then you will re-enter single society as a respected mother and a desirable potential wife. What man would not want a woman whose womb has proved so fecund? But if you have been barren and failed to provide your husband with any heirs then you will not appear as an enviable catch. Indeed, the lack of children may well be seen as the reason your husband left you. You will return to your father's household, taking your dowry with you (subject to any deductions for adulterous behaviour). This is not as bad as it might seem. When your father dies you will inherit and be free to do as you please. You might decide to take over his business affairs or amuse yourself with various love affairs. Whatever path you choose, I have no doubt that you will eventually overcome the disappointment of your failure to be what every good wife must become: a mother.

·· COMMENTARY ··

The family was the basic unit of Roman society and the father sat at its head. He had a duty to protect those within the household but also to guide and discipline them. His family was expected to show him deference and obedience. The state was often seen as simply the household structure writ large, with the senators acting as the fathers of the state. One of the most significant titles of the first emperor, Augustus, was *pater patriae*, 'father of the state', which symbolised his total power over his subjects and his right to intervene in all aspects of their lives.

While the father was probably fairly hands-off for the first few years of his children's lives, he was expected to actively direct his sons' education (see Seneca *On Providence* 2.5; Quintilian *Institutes of Oratory* 1.1.4–6 and 1.4–5). One fascinating text from the first century AD that, apart from a few fragments, survives only in a later Arabic translation, is Bryson Arabus's *Management of the Estate*. This details the father's involvement in all aspects in the running of his household, from raising the sons, to farming, to managing the slaves and choosing a wife (and is now available in translation with detailed commentary by Simon Swain). Of course, this was a text for the rich. Whether it reflected how ordinary Romans thought is impossible to say.

Roman male attitudes to women were condescending at best. They could hold wives in the highest regard (see Pliny the Younger *Letters* 4.19 or the eulogy known as the *Laudatio Turiae*, 'In Praise of Turia') and often worshipped their mothers. But women were also seen as naturally inferior, designed specially for the purposes of childbirth and bringing up children. As Plutarch's *Marriage Precepts* make clear, women were expected to play second fiddle to their husbands in all respects. Some of the stranger male writings about pregnancy are to be found in Soranus's *Gynaecology*. Lucian mocks some of these in his account of life on the moon (*True History* 1.22).

Mortality rates were extremely high in the Roman world, especially in an urban environment, with comparative evidence suggesting that almost a third of children perished within their first year of life and that more than half were dead by the age of ten. This hard but simple fact meant that Roman women were under enormous societal pressure to reproduce. The average woman needed to produce five or six live births, not including miscarriages and stillbirths, just to keep the population level stable. Many women died in childbirth meaning that stepmothers were a common phenomenon, and it was assumed that they would favour their own children to ones they had inherited from a husband's former wife (see, for example, Artemidorus *The Interpretation of Dreams* 3.26 and *The Aesop Romance* 37).

A child did not exist legally until the father accepted the infant into his household, which usually took place on the eighth or ninth day after birth. Prior to that, it was completely at the discretion of the father whether to throw the baby away. This is shocking to us but in a world where there was no form of birth control other than the rhythm method, abortion was probably just as dangerous as childbirth. We can therefore understand abandonment as a form of post-partum abortion. Even today, people disagree passionately about the point at which human life begins, whether abortion is acceptable or at what point abortion should be legally permissible. In Rome, the acceptable dividing line came after the act of birth. Seneca describes how some fathers throw out weak and deformed babies rather than keep them (*Controversies* 10.4.16) but others simply refer to them being born under what was considered to be unlucky alignments of the stars (see, for example, Firmicus Maternus *Eight Books of Astrology* 1.7.20). It is sometimes assumed that these abandoned infants were picked up by those wanting slaves but many also seem to have been eaten by dogs (e.g. Firmicus Maternus 7.2.9, 11, 12, 13, 20, 21).

It is probably reasonable to assume that a majority of exposure was carried out against girls. One surviving letter from Egypt has an absent father telling his pregnant wife what to do if she gives birth before he returns: 'If it is a boy keep it, if it is a girl expose it' (*P. Oxy.* 744). But it is impossible to know how common the practice of exposing infants was. Some archaeological finds suggest a throwaway mentality but these may be related to particular sites, such as brothels. References to exposure are also quite rare. It used to be thought that exposure was more common in Roman Egypt. Many people had what are called copronyms – so-called because copros is Greek for 'dung', so it's like being called Mr Manure – because they had been thrown away at birth. However, since these names were handed down through the generations it seems that they came to act simply as names and cannot be taken as an index of the frequency of exposure.

Between age five and ten seems to have been the most common age for a non-elite child to be sent to work. The collection of Roman law, *Digest* (7.7.6.1), has children working by five. See Bradley, K., *Discovering the Roman Family: Studies in Roman Social History* (Oxford University Press, 1991). The discussion of the repeal of the Oppian law can be found in Livy's *History of Rome* 34.2–4. Rants about the alleged moral decline of women can be read in Seneca *Moral Letters* 95.20–1 and, most famously, Juvenal's sixth satire. Cicero describes the difficult marriage of his brother in his *Letters to Atticus* 5.1, while Augustine refers to the effects and seeming normality of domestic violence (*Confessions* 9.9).

CHAPTER VI

THE PURSUIT OF HAPPINESS

HUNTING, BATHING, PLAYING, laughing – that's living! As the old saying tells us, the good life is a life devoted to leisure. No matter how wealthy you are, if you are a true Roman you will want to enjoy your fair share of the benefits that empire has brought us. Here I shall tell you how to live a fulfilled and fun-filled life.

Rome's excellent form of government allows most people to live in peace and enjoyment. Unlike democracy, which gives free rein to the people's dissolute and uncontrolled desires, our system delivers stability and good sense. Long ago we realised that you cannot run an empire by committee and so turned over its administration to one man, as we would a household to a single father. Ever since Augustus assumed absolute authority and became the leading senator, our government has been a model of justice and efficiency. Never has a people thrived or prospered so much as the Romans under the rule of their emperors.

In a state like Rome, which is governed by its best men, it is inevitable that its citizens are the happiest of all. Freed from all cares and anxieties, they entrust the protection of their leisure to others, whose duty it is to guard it vigilantly. The people can relax in the knowledge that their betters are protecting their interests. As a senator, I am one of those best men. My life is one of leisure in that I have no need to work. Yet I am busier than almost anyone. I take care to live in the public eye. I spend time in the forum and open the doors of my villa for all manner of callers who wish to have an audience with me. When I have nothing to do I make sure I do something and am seen to be doing it. My life of leisure is far from leisurely. You do not have such worries. Instead, you can relax and enjoy the full range of leisure activities that the great city of Rome has to offer.

When asked by a foreigner why he bathed once a day, the emperor is said to have replied, 'Because I do not have the time to bathe twice a day.' I heartily agree. And if you visit one of the magnificent imperial bath complexes so will you. Let me describe those of Titus, by way of example. The entranceway is high and has a wide flight of shallow steps so as not to exhaust those walking up them. You enter into a very spacious hall that provides a large area for slaves and other attendants to wait while their masters bathe. To the left of this hall are elegant and well-lit private rooms, which can be used for the reception of important visitors. Beyond this are two spacious locker rooms that lead on to another hall containing three cold-water pools. The surfaces throughout are decorated with slabs of Laconian marble and white marble statues stand in judicious spots.

When you leave this hall you enter a long oval room that is warm but not so warm as to hit you with a wall of intense heat. Next comes a bright chamber that has been suitably arranged for masseurs to rub you down with oil. A doorway surrounded with Phrygian marble welcomes those coming in from the exercise area outside. The most beautiful of all the rooms, it is designed for whiling away time in relaxation or chatting with your friends. It also gleams with multicoloured marbles. From here you pass into a hot room, whose walls are resplendent with purple. Inside there are three hot tubs. Once you can bear the heat no longer, you leave and enter a cold room. Every room is well proportioned and is radiant with sunlight and good taste. The complex also contains two latrines and two devices for telling the time, one of which is a sundial, the other a loud water clock.

You will find whatever you want in the great imperial baths: washing, a massage, poetry readings, pleasant gardens to take a walk in, libraries and food outlets. Sadly, not all bath houses are so salubrious. After all, what is bathing when you think about it: nothing but oil, sweat, filth and greasy water. The noise can be deafening. When muscle men are swinging about their lead weights the air is filled with groans and gasps. When someone is having a cheap massage, you hear flesh being pummelled. Or there will be a quarrelsome drunk or a thief who has been caught or someone who just loves to sing in the baths, all of which is accompanied by the great splashes of people jumping in the water. Even worse than all this are the men having the hair plucked from their armpits and legs and the endless shouts of hawkers selling their drinks, sausages and pastries, each with his own recognisable cry. And then there is the muscle woman. First she works out with weights, and then she goes to get touched up by the masseur who runs his hands along her thighs. Finally, she heads for the hot room where she loves to sit sweating in the midst of a noisy crowd of men. She'll drink two large glasses of wine on an empty stomach just to sharpen her appetite and then will throw it all up so that she can start again. Disgusting.

As if that isn't bad enough, you'll be pestered by people looking for an invitation to dinner and a free meal at your expense. They'll flatter you and pick up your towel for you, which, even though it's filthier than a baby's bib, they will claim is whiter than snow. While you are combing your thinning hair they will liken your locks to the luxuriant tresses of Achilles. They will wipe your sweaty brow. Eventually, when you have endured a thousand of these tedious tricks, you will give in and invite them round.

Baths also have a seamier side. Theft is a common problem since your discarded clothes offer an easy target for a would-be thief, particularly if your slaves are slack in keeping guard over them. It reminds me of a joke I once heard: while in a bath house, a wit was asked by two different men for the loan of a scraper. One of them was a stranger, the other he knew to be a thief. So he said to the first man, 'Sorry, but I don't know you,' but to the second, 'Sorry, but I do know you!' And then there are those who go looking for amorous adventures. There's one old traditionalist I know, who shall remain name-less, who is always criticising new fashions and anything else un-Roman, but when we bathe together his line of vision keeps below waist level as he devours the young men with his eyes. I read one piece of graffiti at the local baths recently which said, 'Apelles, the emperor's chamberlain, and Dexter had a pleasant lunch here and screwed at the same time.' Even the emperor's valets are up to it!

After bathing, you should be sure to have a good meal. Invite friends round if possible, rather than the sycophants of the bath house. It is a perennial hazard of life in Rome that people receive so many invitations that you will often find yourself stood up by one or more of your guests. This is intensely annoying and I often write to them the following morning to express my discontent. I'll be all mock serious and say that it's outrageous they should make an arrangement to come to dinner and then never show up. I threaten to bill them for the expense I went to cooking the food and opening the wine. I list what had been prepared: a lettuce, three snails, two eggs and a barley cake, along with sea urchins, sows' bellies, sweet wine and even some snow (do you know how expensive that is?). Then there were the olives, beetroot, gourds, onions and a thousand other equally tasty morsels, to say nothing of the entertain-ment. Poetry readers, musicians and dancers from Cadiz had all been employed. They may have dined somewhere more sophisticated, I say, but they will not have had an evening that was more fun, simple or relaxed.

I always try to keep my dinners restrained. We can

have no better example in this than the great emperor Augustus. He always ate sparingly and plainly. He loved coarse bread, fresh cheese made from cow's milk and green figs. He did not wait for mealtimes but ate small quantities whenever he felt hungry. In one of his letters, which I have seen in the senate archive, he writes about this manner of eating: 'I ate a little bread and some small dates, in my carriage.' In another he says, 'When I returned home in my litter, I ate an ounce of bread, and a few raisins.' On one occasion he describes his eating habits at the bath: 'No Jew, my dear Tiberius, ever keeps such a strict fast upon the Sabbath as I have today. While I was at the baths I only ate two biscuits and was then rubbed down with oil.' His indifference to grand dinners was such that he would even sometimes dine alone. Or he would eat before his dinner guests had arrived or after they had left so that he could devote all his attention to talking to them at the table without ever even touching a morsel.

Sadly, our emperors also give us many examples of how not to eat. Vitellius's appetite was as large as his reign was brief. He was addicted to luxury and excess. He always ate three meals a day, sometimes four. On those occasions he would have breakfast, lunch, supper and then a drunken feast to finish with. He was able to cope with eating so much because he had a habit of frequently vomiting. To lower the cost of his fine dining he would invite himself over to friends and other wealthy men where he would insist that the meals cost a minimum of four hundred thousand sesterces. His brother hosted the most infamous of all these dinners and it is said that he served up no fewer than two thousand fresh fish and seven thousand types of bird and fowl. But Vitellius outdid this dinner at a feast he himself gave. This was the first time he was served a new dish, which had been specially devised for him. Because of its enormous size, it was called 'The Shield of Minerva'. The recipe contained livers of char fish tossed together with the brains of pheasants and peacocks, the tongues of flamingos, and the entrails of lampreys caught in the Carpathian Sea and shipped to Rome immediately. Not only did Vitellius have a gargantuan appetite but he would also sometimes eat the most inappropriate things. Once he was attending a sacrifice and he snatched the meat of the bull from the fire and stuffed it into his mouth. Or he would eat any garbage that happened to come his way. So once when he was travelling he stayed at a simple inn and ate the cold, half-eaten leftovers from the day before.

Such excess is to be avoided. I do, however, insist on two things at table: good garum and decent wine. The best garum is made in the following way. The entrails of fish are placed in a vat and salted in the ratio of nine parts fish to one part salt. You can also use small fish, such as tiny mullets, small sprats or anchovies, but the best results will be obtained by using the innards of tuna fish, including the blood and gills. Salt the whole mixture and place it in the sun to age for several months, turning occasionally. Once the fish have fermented and only the small bones are left, strain the mixture through a fine mesh into a vase. The liquid produced has the most wonderful saltiness and will pep up even the plainest food. Do not be tempted to cut corners as so many do and produce a fast garum by simply boiling the fish until they have dissolved. Likewise, when it comes to wine, never opt to serve up the cheap vinegar know as posca, which the lads on the street drink. The finest wines come from Falernia and can improve for many years. Mind you, you should remember that nothing experiences a greater increase in value than Falernian wine that has been cellared for up to twenty years or a greater decrease in value afterwards. So remember to drink it!

Private leisure of this kind cannot compete with the great public games. Everyone loves the gladiators in the Colosseum, the animal hunts, the chariot racing in the Circus Maximus and the shows in the theatre, all of which are provided for the people's entertainment. You should acquaint yourself with all these if you wish to develop more Roman attitudes. Above all you should learn to value such spectacles highly, more highly even than basic commodities like food. The great emperor Trajan, who pacified the warlike people of Dacia, paid a lot of attention to actors and other theatre artists, to the chariot racing and to the fights in the arena because he understood that the people were obsessed with such things. They were interested in the supply of cheap grain that he as emperor gave them but it was not their passion. Trajan knew that his popularity did not rest only on giving the people serious things but also on providing a share in the life of leisure that had traditionally been the preserve of the wealthy. Food is a staple, but the games are the luxury that makes life itself worth living.

If you are lucky enough to be given tickets for the Colosseum – the gladiatorial contests only take place a dozen times a year and are the highlight of the social calendar – you will enjoy a full day's entertainment. You will have to sit according to your social status, which, I am afraid, given that you are a barbarian, is low. This means that you will be sitting in the cheap seats at the top. Even so, you still have an excellent view and it allows you to gaze down on the long rows of spectators cheering and fanatically waving on their favourites.

The morning will begin with the animal hunts. These are extremely popular. Sometimes exotic animals from the farthest reaches of the empire will be displayed, such as giraffes and hippopotamuses. Or bulls will sometimes be made to fight a bear. But mostly, a variety of beasts will be pursued by trained hunters. These men dress in brightly coloured costumes that leave their muscly bodies on display. They go right up close to the animals and often escape seems impossible. But through sheer intelligence and nerve, to say nothing of some well-placed wooden hoardings, the men succeed. Then, when the animals have tired, they spear them or hit them mercilessly with their arrows until they fall. They take care that all the action takes place out in the middle so that everyone can see it. The sheer number of animals can be quite overwhelming if you are not used to it. At one extravagant show put on to celebrate the completion of the emperor's first decade in power, I saw sixty wild boars fight together and among the many other beasts that were slain were an elephant and a corocotta. The corocotta is an Indian species and this was the first time it had ever been seen in Rome. It looks like a lion crossed with a tiger but also has something of the look of a dog and a fox, all curiously blended into one animal. As the highlight of the show, the entire arena was made to resemble a boat in shape. Suddenly, the sides of the 'ship' came apart and hundreds of animals came rushing out from within it. Bears, panthers, lions, ostriches, wild asses, bison, as well as all kinds of domestic animals, were seen running about terrified as the hunters steadily picked them off with their bows. The slaughter was magnificent to behold.

The emperor Titus specialised in this kind of spectacular show. In one, a battle between great birds and four elephants took place. In the games he held to celebrate the opening of the Colosseum, nine thousand animals were killed and even women took part in the slaughter, as did armed dwarfs. Instead of simple fights between individual gladiators, he arranged for pitched battles between hundreds of infantry and had the arena flooded to recreate a naval combat. The games continued for a hundred days and he even offered the people material benefits besides the visual ones on display. He created a lottery by having attendants throw small wooden balls into the crowd. On them would be inscribed the prize the lucky holder of the ball would receive: it might be some food, or new clothing, or a silver cup or even a gold one, or horses, pack animals or slaves. Needless to say, the competition to grab one of these balls was intense and many were crushed to death in the stampedes.

Lunchtime offers some light relief with the executions. Recently I saw a bandit called Selurus executed because he had led a small uprising near Etna in Sicily. He was placed on top of a high scaffold, which had been decorated to resemble Etna itself. All of a sudden this collapsed and he fell into a cage of wild beasts that promptly ripped him apart. It was an amusing and suitable end for a man who had himself behaved like a wild animal on the side of the volcano. Some people find these punishments hard to stomach, but you should remember that physical punishment is natural for those at the bottom of society. It is right that it takes place in public so that everyone can see that the guilty are paying for their offences with their pain. You will have to brush up on your mythology since the executions often make use of it to create entertaining tableaux. I once saw a condemned criminal called Laureolus being bound to a rock as if he were Prometheus who, as you may remember, had a vulture feed on his innards for all eternity. This Laureolus, suspended on a cross, had his entrails fed to a Scottish bear. His mangled limbs quivered, and every part of his shapeless body dripped with gore. And on another occasion a prisoner emerged from underground into the arena carrying a lyre as if he were Orpheus. All around him were lions and other wild animals, who initially seemed to be tamed by his music as they were in the myth. Just when the criminal was starting to believe this himself, at a given signal the animals turned upon him and tore him apart. It was very wittily done.

After the executions comes the highlight of the day: the gladiators. The emperor will take his seat before the cheering crowd as the fighters are led in. In preparation for the fights, you see swords being sharpened, metal plates being heated up to be used to check that the fallen gladiators are not pretending to be dead, and rods and whips are produced to drive timid gladiators on against their opponents. Trumpets blare out to signal that the contests are about to begin. Then the fights commence.

What shouts go up as each fighter thrusts and parries the other's blows. What cries and groans go with the inevitable wounds. You will find it utterly fascinating. Best of all is when a fallen gladiator raises his finger and asks for mercy. You can hear a pin drop. Then everyone will erupt into a flurry of cheering or booing, shaking their togas and indicating whether the emperor's thumb should be turned up or down. The emperor knows how to milk the moment. This is decision time and all eyes are on him. He will wait to see what the crowd wants, then keep them in suspense a little longer. Finally, he gives his decision with a dramatic gesture, clearly visible to all. Mercy means that the gladiator lives to fight another day. But if he has failed to win over the crowd then he must meet his fate like a man. Throwing his head back to expose his neck, he must receive the downward thrust of his opponent's sword with all his body. In death he can redeem his failure in life.

Most gladiators might start as the scum of the earth – slaves and condemned criminals – but you can learn much from them. They will teach you the military traditions and love of discipline that made Rome great. Their bravery and skill is what all men should aspire to. In their indifference to death we see the self-sacrifice that any Roman should be prepared to make for his country. It all shows that Rome is capable of turning any miserable barbarian into a model of manly virtue. Gladiators are the epitome of self-improvement.

You can overdo it, though. There is nothing so damaging to developing good character than lounging around endlessly at the games. It is when we are at leisure that vice is most able to sneak up on us. This is particularly true of some of the lesser-quality shows. Hunting, for example, should show wit, skill and creativity. If there is nothing but slaughter where is the gain in that? Some of the midday executions in particular can be very dreary. The condemned men will have no means of protecting themselves against the onrushing beasts or have no armour to keep off the blows of opponents. When there is no protection there can be no skill. The worst kind of spectator seems to enjoy this. 'Kill him! Whip him! Burn him!' they shout. They just want to see death for its own sake when it should be used as a way of displaying the highest qualities a man has to offer. So to keep them entertained, some simple throat cutting takes place in the interludes just to fill up the time. Of course, the criminals deserve to die – they are all robbers and murderers, after all. But the games should be about more than that: they should be a display of the skill, courage and grace under pressure that made Rome what it is. When you look at the dregs of the crowd it makes you despair for the future.

It is horrific how the common people relax and have fun in the streets or dingy taverns and you must not copy their example. The poorest of them spend the whole night in bars or they hang out in the arches around the theatre. You see them arguing with each other about their dice games and they habitually make a disgusting noise by snorting their breath back into their nostrils.

Their favourite pastime is to stand about for the whole day – from dawn to dusk and whatever the weather – discussing in endless detail the good and bad points of the charioteers and horses that are due to run in the Circus Maximus. Once they are packed together to see the races, the crowd is a truly remarkable sight to behold: innumerable masses of plebs, with their minds taken over by a passion for the chariot racing. This is why you cannot do anything serious in Rome any more. I am astonished that so many thousands of grown men should have such a childish obsession with some horses galloping about and a few men standing in chariots. I could understand it if it were the speed of the horses or the skill of the charioteers which attracted them. But in fact they are interested only in the stable they race for because that's what they bet on. So if any of the competitors changed their colours in mid-race all the fans would instantly abandon them for another and scream their support for them instead.

Taverns can be dangerous places. All kinds of low life dwell there and it is well known that all the women who work in them can be hired as prostitutes. This dreadful reputation also means that the authorities keep a close eye on them. I have heard of reckless men who were trapped by undercover soldiers in the following manner. A soldier in civilian clothing sits down beside you and then begins to criticise the emperor in the strongest terms. You think you are safe to speak your mind because your drinking companion started it and so you launch into your own tirade. And before you know it, you are being handcuffed and led away, never to be seen again.

Do not gamble excessively. Romans love gambling even though it is illegal, apart from at dinner parties and during the festival of the Saturnalia, when even the lowliest slave can shake his dice-box with impunity. Go into any tavern and you will find a gaming board. You even see these boards put up outside to entice customers, but letters are used instead of squares so that it is not obvious that the law is being broken. They then use these letters to spell out supposedly funny sayings. I saw one recently which said:

> IGNORE WEALTH
> INSANE GREED
> TURNS MINDS

Very ironic, no doubt. Or they might even mock the players themselves:

> LEAVE YOUR SEAT
> YOU CAN'T PLAY
> GET LOST IDIOT

Charming. Another one seemed at least to understand the truth of Roman leisure:

> WITH THE BRITS CONQUERED
> AND THE PERSIANS KILLED
> PLAY ON YOU ROMANS

It's because we have conquered the world that we Romans can afford to spend so much time having fun. For the poor people this is because the emperor in his magnanimity grants each male citizen a monthly handout of free grain to help feed his family. Of course the downside is that the great Roman people, who used to decide on important matters of state, such as whether to go to war, is now only interested in two things: bread and circuses.

You can pick up all kinds of bad habits in gambling. The common people argue so much because they are always trying to cheat each other. They'll claim that they threw a pair when in fact it was a three. Or they will use magical spells. I was playing a game at dinner once when one of my freedmen started muttering into the hand which was holding the dice he was about to throw: 'Make me a winner dice, O powerful god, THERTHENITHOR DYAGOTHERE THERTHENITHOR SYAPOTH-EREUO KODOCHOR. Let no one be equal to me, for I am THERTHENITHOR EROTHORTHIN DOLOTHOR, and I am going to throw what I want.' He kept on repeating this every time he threw until we all starting laughing so much at him that he grew embarrassed and stopped.

As is so often the case, you should model yourself on the great emperor, Augustus. He loved to play but he didn't show the slightest concern about whether he won or not. He played a game where every individual puts in a denarius if he throws an ace or a six, with the winner taking it all if he throws a Venus, which is a throw containing one of each number. It was normal for him to lose twenty thousand a night because he was always letting his guests win, and would even give them a few hundred denarii to use as stake money.

Leisure is both a boon and a danger. We all know that the young person who inherits too much wealth is likely to have life made too easy for him and he soon grows lazy and apathetic because he has nothing left to pursue or desire. So too you, if you are to be a true Roman, will have to control your inner vices. For once you are as successful as the Romans are, you will be exposed to all manner of luxury, which can quickly corrupt the mind and cause your character to degenerate.

Luxury first came to Rome when Manlius Vulso celebrated his triumph over the Asiatic Gauls. He had let his troops engage in all kinds of excessive behaviour and, like a plague, they brought it back with them when they returned to Rome. They carried with them a fat booty, the likes of which had never before been seen: bronze couches, costly tapestries and other soft fabrics, and silver salvers. They held banquets where girls played on the harp, sang and danced, and the food was prepared with great care and expense. Suddenly the humble cook, who the Romans had always viewed as the lowliest of slaves, began growing in both status and cost. What had once been regarded as a menial job was now seen as a fine art. Still, this was as nothing compared with the torrent of luxury that was to later consume the city.

I have with my own eyes seen a lover of a previous emperor attend a wedding feast covered with interlaced emeralds and pearls – all over her head, her hair, ears, neck and hands – worth a sum total of forty million sesterces. These were not presents from the emperor. They were family heirlooms that had long ago been acquired in the conquest of foreign provinces. Originally taken as bribes from a foreign king, the jewels now decorated a woman who was behaving no better than a harlot. Either way, the gems go to show the pernicious ability of luxury to corrupt, whatever the age or sex of those exposed to it. And this is by no means the worst example I have come across. Cleopatra owned the two largest pearls in world history, having inherited them from her father. When Mark Antony was gorging himself every day at lavish banquets, Cleopatra arrogantly laughed at him: 'You call that splendour?' she said, 'I could spend 10 million sesterces on a single feast!' Antony was fascinated to know how so much money could be spent on a single meal, and he had several bets with people, believing that it could not be done.

The next day, Cleopatra set before Antony a fine banquet. It was a splendid affair, with the very best aged wines and choicest cuts of meat, and the queen presided wearing her finest jewels, including those two huge pearls as earrings. But in truth it was no more than Antony had become used to throwing every day. He laughed at its meanness. But the queen insisted that the bill for the meal would hit eight figures and she then ordered a second course to be served. As he had been instructed, a servant entered carrying only a single glass into which he poured some strong vinegar. Antony leaned forward, curious to see what Cleopatra was going to do. She removed one earring and dropped the pearl into the vinegar, which quickly dissolved it. She then drank it. Lucius Plancus, who was acting as judge to decide whether or not the bet had been won, stopped Cleopatra when she made to repeat this with her other earring. 'Antony has lost the battle,' he declared – ominously, given what was to later transpire when Antony and Cleopatra fought Augustus at Actium. Indeed, after that defeat, and Cleopatra's subsequent suicide, the second pearl was taken to Rome and cut in two so that its two colossal halves could decorate the ears of a statue of the goddess Venus which stood in the Pantheon.

If anyone ever tells you that great riches are a blessing, reply that they should learn from the story of the country mouse. Once upon a time a mouse had a visit from a city mouse, who was an old friend of his. The country mouse lived in a small cave and had only a few simple possessions within its walls, but he was hospitable to his guests when he had them. He did not begrudge giving his urban friend the turnips he had carefully stored up for the winter, or the oats. He even served up a dry plum and nibbled scraps of bacon, thinking that foods such as these would be more to the liking of his friend's sophisticated palate, while the host himself dined on simple grains of spelt. Eventually, the city mouse said to him, 'Why do you live such a hard life on the edge of a harsh forest? Wouldn't you have a better time if you moved to the town with all its conveniences? Take my advice and come back with me and see what you are missing. You only live once and it's a short life at that.'

The country mouse was persuaded and off the two friends went and by nightfall they had crept under the city gates. The city mouse led them to a gorgeous palace, where the floors were covered with carpets dyed crimson and ivory couches glittered with gold decoration. On the table sat the remains of a sumptuous feast from the evening before. It was the city mouse's turn to be host and he scurried about bringing his guest fine food from the abandoned dishes. Happily he reclined and told his guest stories of urban life. Suddenly, a door opened with a terrible rattling. The two terrified mice scampered all over the room looking for an exit while the sound of barking dogs grew closer and closer. Luckily, they found a small crack in the base of a wall and escaped from their terrible pursuers. As they left the palace, the country mouse turned to his friend and said, 'Goodbye, my friend. I do not want to live like this. My simple wood, safe from all surprises, is home comfort enough for me.'

The tale warns us not to be taken in by the fast pace and luxuries of city life. But it also tells us of the benefits of friendship. In our brief spell on this earth, we should always be on the lookout for individuals whom we can love and who will love us in return. For goodwill and affection are the principal joys of life. My dear friend, Scipio, for example, will always live with me even though death suddenly snatched him away. His virtue lives on in all of us and inspires anyone who is looking to achieve something great in life. These are the kind of friends you need: loyal, principled and virtuous. That is not what most men look for in their friends. They want their friends to compensate for their own deficiencies and expect them to display qualities that they themselves do not possess. Be a good man yourself and then try to find others like you. If you are successful, you will become united with them by ties of goodwill and they will never give in to the passions of envy and greed to which most other men are slaves. Instead, your true friends will delight in being your equal and will go to any lengths to help you, secure in the knowledge that you will do likewise for them if needs be. They will never ask you to do anything dishonourable or unfair and they will both cherish and love you. It is not too much to say that true friends have the deepest respect for each other. Whoever receives such respect from a friendship is the recipient of its brightest jewel.

My longest-standing friend is Vestricius Spurinna and I do not think I have ever spent a more delightful time than during my recent visit to his estate. Though very old, he serves as a model of how to live the good life. I love men who plan their lives with the regularity of the movements of the stars. A little disorder and rush is forgivable in a young man but for older men, whose days of such exertion and ambition are past, a calm and well-ordered life is by far the most suitable. This is how Spurinna lives. He moves through his days like a moon in orbit. In the morning he stays in bed until about the second hour, when he will call for his slaves to bring his shoes and help dress him. He then goes on a three-mile walk. On his return, he will have a slave read a book out loud to him. If he has friends staying in the house, he will ask them to join him and the time passes in discussions on the most noble of topics. What stories of the good old days you hear. What noble deeds and noble men he tells you about. But he is so modest and unassuming that you never feel you are being given a lecture, even though you are learning more than you ever did at school.

Next on Spurinna's schedule is a seven-mile ride followed by another walk of a mile. After this, he retires to his study where he composes lyric poetry of the most scholarly fashion in both Greek and Latin metre. If you are lucky, he will read them to you – they have such grace, wit and charm. When he is told that the bathing hour has come – this is the ninth hour in winter and the eighth in summer – he takes a walk naked in the sun, so long as there is no wind. Then he exercises with a ball, and throws himself into the game because he understands how exercise of this kind helps battle against the forces of old age. After his bath, he lies down and waits a little while before eating. Dinner is then served, with the table being presented in a light but restrained manner. The silver is plain and old-fashioned and the food is served on tasteful Corinthian pottery. The dinner is often accompanied by actors who recite comic verse to keep the atmosphere light. The meal lasts well into darkness but never seems to drag. Finally, the host will retire, never having overindulged in either food or wine. As a result of his lifestyle, Spurinna is a model of health and happiness even though he is nearly seventy-seven years old. His hearing and eyesight are perfect, his body active and his mind alert. The only symptom of his age is his wisdom. This is the sort of life we should all aspire to lead once we have put aside the cares of business and public life.

It reminds me of the great Manius Curius, who, having defeated the Samnites, the Sabines and King Pyrrhus, spent his final years in simple rural frugality. What character he displayed. When the Samnites had brought him a great mass of gold as tribute, he scornfully rejected their gift: 'There is no glory in gold,' he said, 'only in ruling those who have it.' Those were the days before urban living had wrought its corrupting influence upon the Roman spirit. Back then senators lived on farms. The great Quinctius Cincinnatus was working at the plough when he was notified of his election to the dictatorship. What reason was there to pity the old age of men like him, who delighted in farming the soil? I believe that no life can be happier than a farmer's. His work benefits the entire human race, his life is full of rural charm, and nature rewards his efforts with an abundance that makes him revere the gods. His cellars are always brimful of oil and wine, and his household full of the smells of pork, goat meat, lamb, poultry, cheese and honey. And that is to say nothing of the harvest of the kitchen garden and the fruits of hawking and hunting.

However you take your pleasures, modesty and restraint must always predominate. Even literature – which is, after all, the most becoming activity for a gentleman to spend time and money on – is only acceptable if kept under control. What is the use of owning so many books that the owner has no chance of ever reading them all? It is much better to devote yourself to a few writers than to skim through many. When the great library at Alexandria burned down, forty thousand books were lost. Did it matter? Such a vast library had nothing to do with taste or learning but was a piece of extravagant luxury built by an oriental king to show off his supposed love of letters. You should use books to help you learn, not to decorate your dining room. What excuse is there to buy bookcases made of ivory or citrus wood and fill them with the works of orators and historians if they are not to be read? People treat knowledge as if it were a gold tap, something bought for display.

The unhappy man is he who is made dull through excessive pleasure, a man whose sluggish contentment keeps him becalmed in a flat sea. Happiness is living in tune with nature. Since nature will always throw up various misfortunes and disasters, we must learn how to cope with these rough waters. We must learn not to be dragged about by fate but to go along with it. You must discipline your desires. Wealth will please you all the more if you can also delight in simplicity. You should never waste money on trying to impress others but spend it only on things that deliver a practical benefit. Buy food sufficient to tame your hunger, drink enough to slake your thirst. Contain your lusts within the limits of need. Live like the ancients and adopt a lifestyle that does not follow the costly vagaries of contemporary fashion. Control your desires and your pleasures and repress any urge to indulge in luxury. Do not condemn the poor for their poverty but learn instead to live in unashamed thrift. The greatest wealth lies within your soul and can be unlocked by your own self-control. You will never defeat fortune or avoid all of the vast range of calamities she can send your way. But the yoke always feels heaviest to the softest neck and only those who have experienced misfortune can ever really know true happiness.

·· COMMENTARY ··

Most of our surviving texts from the Roman world were written by men drawn from the highest echelons of society. Only the wealthiest could afford the many years of expensive education it took to learn the rhetorical and literary skills needed to produce literature of the highest calibre. In such a world, it is perhaps not surprising to find that these men held themselves in high esteem, particularly with regard to their ability to govern Rome for the benefit of all its citizens (see, for example, Cicero *Republic* 1.34). This was despite the fact that the late republic was torn apart by factionalism between competing aristocrats, who sought to maximise their own glory and power through conquest and political office. We would be more cynical about our politicians, and would find such paternalism condescending at best. We have no evidence for what ordinary Romans thought about high-ranking politicians such as Cicero because their views were not considered important enough to record for posterity. The fact that so many Roman citizens served loyally in the armies – possibly more in percentage terms than in any other pre-industrial state – does not suggest that they were at odds with their political leaders. Military service provided opportunities for glory and personal gain. When generals such as Pompey or Julius Caesar gave their soldiers end-of-campaign bonuses they were worth several years' pay.

The wealth which empire concentrated in the city of Rome allowed this political elite, and later the emperors, to lavish enormous sums on providing the citizenry with subsidised grain and spectacular entertainment. The imperial baths were huge leisure complexes and those who have seen the colossal walls of the baths of Caracalla will have got a sense of the scale of these establishments. The description above is based on that of Lucian's *Hippias*, which is a eulogy on the benefits of bathing. Seneca's *Letters* 56 contains a graphic account of all the noises emanating from a bath house. Martial's epigrams contain numerous examples of alleged immoralities taking place in the hot and steamy atmosphere of the bath house. Pliny (*Letters* 1.15) complains about a friend who has not turned up for dinner and threatens to charge him for it. The *Geoponica*, a tenth-century Byzantine collection of folklore, contains several recipes for garum, the fish sauce that the Romans used widely to add some kick to their food.

Augustine's *Confessions* contains the famous account of his young Christian friend being seduced by the thrill and excitement of the games. Fronto (*Letters* 2.18.9–17) explains the political principles behind putting on the games for the people. The accounts of Severus's games and those of Titus can be found in Dio Cassius *History of Rome* (66.25 and 77.1). Examples of criminals being executed as part of a re-enactment of a mythological scene can be found in Strabo *Geography* 6.2 and Martial *On the Spectacles* 7. Seneca (*Letters* 5) argues that nothing is so bad for the character as lounging at the games and particularly condemns the rabble that watches the gruesome midday executions, but we should be careful not to see this as reflecting the general view. Part of the point of Seneca's text is to display his form of Stoicism, which held a certain sympathy with all human beings, regardless of their status. Even then, he does not think the condemned criminals did not deserve to die, just that the Roman crowd would benefit from higher-minded executions than simple butchery. On the games as a whole and for further reading, see my *The Day Commodus Killed a Rhino: Understanding the Roman Games* (Johns Hopkins University Press, 2014).

The account of the plebs' gambling is based on Ammianus Marcellinus's description of the fourth-century people of Rome (14.6.25–6), while Falx's contempt for the racing factions can be found in Pliny *Letters* 9.6. A spell for use in playing dice can be found in the *Greek Magical Papyri* 7.423–8. The dangers of undercover police are relayed in Epictetus *Dissertations* 4.13.5, although it is impossible to say how widespread such activity was. It does at least show that emperors could be aware that people did not always believe the kind of flattery they habitually served up when face-to-face with their ruler.

The Romans had a slightly hypocritical attitude towards luxury. On the one hand they readily accepted the rewards of empire and spent huge sums on their own benefits. But on the other they often harked back to a mythical golden age when Rome's purity of values was uncorrupted and plain to see (Falx's comments are based primarily on Livy's *History of Rome* 39.6 and Pliny the Elder *Natural History* 9.58.117–18). Perhaps this disquiet reflected a concern that the Roman citizen body, which had won the empire through its legendary toughness, was likely to soften under the influence of the many luxuries Rome had to offer.

Cicero's *On Friendship* offers a detailed account of the high value upper-class Romans placed on friendship, although it is worth noting that this did not often cross social barriers. Cicero himself did free his highly educated slave Tiro (the name, incidentally, for a novice gladiator) and wrote to him almost as an equal (except that he often jokingly threatens to slap him), but this was probably not the norm. Rome's highly stratified society made it very difficult for friendships between men of different levels to thrive for the simple reason that such a relationship would normally have been classed as one of patron and client. Falx's description of his wealthy friend's lifestyle is drawn from Pliny *Letters* 3.1. Cicero's *On Old Age* contains the account of Manius Curius. The power of the image of the farmer-general was such that the American general, George Washington, was often likened to, and portrayed as, the Roman Cincinnatus. Seneca attacks people collecting vast libraries of unread books (*On the Tranquil Mind* 9) and urges the Stoic acceptance of whatever fate sends your way in his *Letters* (48.7–8).

CHAPTER VII

A HEALTHY MIND IN A HEALTHY BODY

I F THERE IS ONE THING you should pray for in this life, it is a healthy mind in a healthy body. A man who has health and vigour will never need the attentions of the medics or even the masseurs or anointers. His life will have variety since he has the strength to travel to his country estates and then to make the return journey to town for business. He will sail, hunt, exercise frequently, but rest only occasionally. Inactivity weakens the body and brings on premature old age, whereas work strengthens it and prolongs youth. If there is one characteristic the Roman people have displayed in abundance, it is their energy. Not content to sit in their home town, they pushed ever further outwards until a great empire lay in their hands. Let me reveal the secrets of how you too can create this vigour in your own self.

I myself have followed a particular lifestyle ever since I was twenty-eight years old. At that time, after a careful study of the writings of the doctors, I realised that there is an art to maintaining your health. I stick to my principles rigidly and have never been sick with any disease since then, apart from a few mild fevers. The lifestyle rests on six essential factors, which all promote health individually but followed together make you almost invincible to illness: diet, exercise, your environment, sleep, the care of the mind, and maintaining a balance through the pursuit of moderation in all things. Nature knows best and understands what your body needs. But if you do not help her then nature struggles.

You must live your life in accordance with nature. You must understand the nature of your own body. Our bodies are collections of different kinds of liquid: black bile, yellow bile, blood and phlegm are the main four although there are others as well, such as sweat, semen, urine and spit. Sickness results primarily from an imbalance among these fluids. But the body also has other characteristics: whether it is lean or fat, hot or cold, moist or dry. In some people, the stool is generally loose, in others firm. The type of illness you suffer will reflect the impact these differences have on the four basic liquids. We all have natural weaknesses that lend themselves to creating imbalance and you should endeavour to counteract this deficiency, whatever it might be. If you are too thin, you must aim to fatten yourself up. A hot man needs to cool himself down, while the constipated need to loosen their bowels. Always direct your attention at that part of you which is most in trouble.

With diet, be particularly careful about how much you eat. The body is best able to digest an amount of food that is proportionate to its size. If you stuff yourself full then the body will leave large quantities undigested, which will impede the action of the gut. One simple way to tell if your body is sound is to look at your morning urine. If it is whitish, then later in the morning reddish, this means that digestion is still taking place and that you have eaten excessively the evening before.

It is best to start a meal with small savouries or salads, after which you should eat either boiled or roast meat. Meat, however, is hard to digest and it should not be eaten in excess and, if you are old, not at all. Avoid preserved fruits because of their sweetness, which also makes them hard to digest. Dessert does no harm to a good stomach, but it can turn a weak one sour. If you suffer from a weak stomach, you would do better to eat dates, apples and the like at the start of the meal. Once you have drunk your fill, do not eat any more as it distends the gut. Likewise, do not exercise after you are full. The best way to end the meal is with a glass of cold water, after which you should try to stay awake for a while before sleeping in order to allow your body a chance to begin digestion.

For everyone, wine is best drunk in moderation. In excess it can make otherwise sensible people angry, impulsive and aggressive. It also turns the rational part of the brain sluggish and confused. Wine is especially good for the elderly as it greatly helps improve the function of the kidneys. It is best avoided by the young, who are hot-headed enough as it is.

If you are too thin and wish to fatten yourself up, follow this plan. Take only moderate exercise, rest more often, have yourself rubbed with oil and take regular baths after the midday meal. Also, restrict your bowel movements to one per day, sleep more and do so on a soft bed. Never allow yourself to get distressed or angry, and eat plenty of suet and fatty foods. Eat meals as large as it is possible to digest and have them regularly. Gladiators offer us the best example of men who put on lots of weight. These 'barley-men', as they are often called, stuff themselves with grains but eat little meat. They soon grow big, which helps them in their contests, as the fat helps protect them against the blows of their opponents. However, gladiators also need to strengthen their bones in order to support such a great increase in weight. They therefore take supplements mixed into their food, such as wood ash or ground animal bone.

If, however, you are too fat and wish to lose weight, you should do the following. Bathe on an empty stomach in hot water, especially if it is salty. Stay out in the hot sun to help dry your body out. Stay up late, make your bed hard and sleep less. Become anxious about every aspect of your life and run, walk and exercise violently. Eat sour and sharp foods but only take a single meal a day. Drink warm wine on an empty stomach.

Vomiting is also a useful way to lose weight as is purging yourself with laxatives. Naturally, you should not vomit daily in order to allow yourself to eat as much as possible at mealtimes. Nor should laxatives be too strong since this can produce a violent effect that is hard to control. But, used in moderation, these means allow you simple ways to expel undesirable matter from your body without reducing its strength. I find that vomiting is more beneficial in winter than in summer, for that is when the body has more phlegm and the head can become stuffy as a result. A good vomit is particularly useful for those who are bilious as a result of over-eating or poor digestion, but it should be avoided by those who are too thin or have a sensitive stomach. So if you have overindulged and are suffering from pain or weight above the heart, you should immediately make yourself vomit. Likewise, if you have heartburn, excessive salivation, nausea, ringing in the ears or a bitter taste in the mouth, vomiting will help. Obviously rest would often be advised as well. But if you are too busy to lie on your couch, then it is a quick and easy remedy. Just remember that no one who wants to live to old age should make it a daily habit.

To make yourself vomit after a meal, first drink tepid water. Once you have drunk enough that it is becoming difficult to take on more, add a little salt or honey to the water. If you want to be sick in the morning, first drink some honey or hyssop in wine or eat a radish followed by tepid water and salt. After you have vomited and the stomach is still upset, eat a little food and, unless the vomiting has made your throat sore, drink three cupfuls of cold water. You should then go for a walk, bathe and have a slave rub you down with oil and then eat. The meal should be light – just some dry bread, roast meat and rough, undiluted wine.

Fasting is something I recommend strongly. Set aside a certain number of days and then restrict yourself to small, plain meals, with no wine. I even dress plainly as well in order to emphasise to myself the simplicity of the period. You will find that doing this when times are good trains you for when fate turns against you. It allows you to toughen your body and your soul so that you can cope with misfortune all the more easily. Just as a soldier trains himself in peace for times of war, so you too should develop the strength of character to cope with poverty and want.

Regular bowel movements are highly desirable. Constipation is often caused by sitting still for too long or by eating too little. If you are constipated take a laxative to loosen the stool. Otherwise you will suffer from an increase in flatulence, dizziness of vision, headaches, and other disturbances in the upper parts. To keep yourself regular, make sure that you ingest certain kinds of food and drink, and keep active: take regular walks, eat more, move about after meals and drink plenty during meals. If your bowels are too loose and you find yourself struggling to make it to the latrine, you should exercise the upper parts of your body by playing such things as handball. Also, walk on an empty stomach, keep out of the sun and do not bathe too often. Avoid eating stews, pulses or greens. Instead, eat venison and hard fish – anything which will pass through you slowly – or roast meat. Never drink wine that has been watered down with seawater, but drink that which is fuller-bodied. Cold drinks are to be taken as often as possible. Whenever you feel that you have eaten something that disagrees with you, make yourself sick immediately, and then do not eat anything except a small quantity of bread soaked in wine and a few preserved grapes for three days. Always rest after a meal and keep your mind relaxed.

If you suffer from excessive flatulence, avoid all manner of cold food and drink and all sweets and pulses. Bad breath is best cured by gargling with red wine that has been well spiced. Ground marble dust can also be added to this. This reminds me of a good joke I heard recently. A man with bad breath went to the doctor and said, 'Look, Doctor, my uvula is lower than it should be.' 'Phew,' gasped the doctor, as the man opened his mouth to show him, 'It's not your uvula that has gone down, it's your arse that has come up!'

Exercise is vital to good health. It also helps avoid fatigue, makes the organs work better, improves breathing and helps remove noxious substances. We can define exercise as that which raises respiration. For some of you, that will mean running or throwing heavy balls in the gymnasium before bathing. For others, it will involve only a brisk walk or deep breathing. Exercise should result in sweating and some tiredness but not excessive fatigue. In general, it is best to avoid exercise immediately before or after a meal. Avoid exercise that is too rapid or violent. Moderation is best and you should learn to recognise when you have done enough. If you are fatigued after exercise, you should rest on the next day and bathe in warm water. Massage is also thoroughly recommended, preferably on a daily basis.

You may be trying to ready yourself to fight in battle. If so, you can have no better model than the training regime of the Roman legions. Initially, you should focus on learning to march quickly in time with others. Nothing is more important than this because in battle success will ultimately depend on the ability of the front line to maintain its formation. I recommend that you aim to march for twenty miles in five hours and then build this up to twenty-four miles. If you are young enough, you should also run for exercise, to enable you to charge the enemy more vigorously or take up an advantageous position more quickly. Jumping and leaping are also excellent exercise, and this ability will help you to cross ditches and such obstacles with ease. It has another great advantage. A soldier who attacks his enemy while running and jumping dazzles him with his speed and agility and fills him with terror. Before he has had time to react, the enemy has been struck down dead by your javelin. Pompey the Great used to swear by such exercises and made his soldiers do them all the time.

Swimming is a definite for the summer months. Then you will be able to cross rivers without bridges. Traditionally, Roman soldiers always exercised on the Campus Martius, north of the city centre, which also lay on the banks of the Tiber, where they would practise their swimming. Have your horses swim too, in case they need to cross some swollen torrent.

The post exercise is an excellent way to improve your fitness. You should arm yourself with a wooden shield and sword, both twice as heavy as actual weapons. Then attack a wooden post as if it were an enemy, sometimes aiming blows at what would be the head or face, other times at the sides or as if you were attacking the thighs. Dance back and forward as you would in a real contest, using your shield to ensure that you do not lay yourself open to attack. Do this repeatedly throughout the day and your fitness will really come on. You won't be surprised to learn that it is a favourite method of training among gladiators.

Vaulting wooden horses used to be widely practised

but has lapsed in these softer times. You should learn to jump the vault first without carrying weapons but then do so fully armed. The aim should be to train yourself to be indifferent as to whether you are mounting the horse from the left or the right, or with the sword in your left or right hand. This is a vital skill for the cavalry to have since in the confusion of battle it often happens that you will have to dismount your horse to kill an enemy but then need to remount with great speed. Finally, you should practise carrying heavy loads. Make yourself carry bags weighing not less than sixty pounds in addition to your armour and weapons. This will simulate the necessity of having to carry provisions as well as arms when on campaign.

You need to keep your mind healthy as well as your body. Indeed, the two are inextricably linked. A healthy and balanced mind helps maintain the body's well-being just as a sound body supports the mind. Someone who is angry or anxious, for example, finds their temperature rising and their breathing becoming irregular. Rage is nothing short of madness and it makes people lash out, kick, rip their clothes and even get angry with doors or keys, which they will shake, kick and even bite. It is like when you see some starving beggar whose mind does not know how to endure the hunger. He accosts us with his pitiful appearance and begs us, but when this fails he resorts to chewing the leather of worn-out shoes or grows insane and hammers nails into his head or dives into freezing water, anything to gather a crowd round him whom he hopes will spare him a crust. You need to train your mind so that it can control such physical pressures.

If your mind is weak or becomes infirm, you should rub your head gently in the morning after breakfast. Do everything you can to keep the head cool and so avoid overheating the brain. Never cover it up with a blanket since this will only increase the heat within. In fact, it is best to shave the head. You should avoid fires and hot baths. Above all, avoid walking in strong sunlight, which is guaranteed to addle the brain. Also keep out of moonlight and never walk anywhere after dinner. Nothing is better for the brain than cold water, so during the summer months you should hold your head under a stream of cold water for several minutes each day. Drink only light wine to avoid the head becoming heavy and water it down to weaken it further. Avoid all arguments and even writing or reading, since all kinds of thinking will only risk aggravating the mind.

The antics of those who have gone insane serve as warning signs to us all. Every town has some poor fool who lives among the tombs, naked, crying or bruising himself with stones. I have seen a man who thought he was Atlas and walked around with hunched shoulders as if he bore the weight of the world on his shoulders. I have seen a woman who believed that the world would end if she bent her finger. One friend of mine became convinced that a snake was living inside his stomach. The doctor cleverly made him vomit but slipped into the bowl a small viper which he then showed to the patient. Immediately the patient was cured, although he did relapse later since he believed that the snake had laid eggs before emerging from his gut.

A form of madness that is peculiar to women is

hysteria. This is an illness arising from the movement of the womb within the woman's body. Found mainly in virgins and widows, and depending on where the womb has moved to within the body, the symptoms include shortness of breath, chest pain, pain in the legs or groin, and seizure. The best treatments are those that try to coax or coerce the wandering womb back into its proper place. Have the doctor apply foul odours to the nose to repel the uterus downwards if it has risen high up into the body. Conversely, fragrant aromas can be applied to the woman's vagina to try to entice the womb into returning to its proper place. With women, it is also important to look for hidden causes. Once a woman lay awake at night, constantly tossing and turning, to the exasperation of other doctors. The great doctor Galen noticed that her pulse quickened whenever he mentioned the name of the heart-throb actor Pylades, and so was able to diagnose love-sickness.

Doctors disagree about the best way to deal with the insane. Many doctors argue that they should be kept in chains or treated with certain tortures. They say that whenever the insane say or do anything wrong, they should be starved, put in fetters or flogged. They believe it is beneficial for the patients to be suddenly terrified and thoroughly frightened. Some doctors treat epilepsy by binding the limbs, or by prescribing potions made from weasel and the testes of a beaver, while others place a flame close to the patient's eye and tickle him. Hellebore is commonly used as a purge to clean out the mind alongside the body. Other doctors argue that the insane should be treated more gently and kept free from stress.

Those who are depressed should go to the theatre and see a comedy, whereas those who are euphoric should be taken to a tragedy. Many people believe that the insane have had their heads occupied by demons and buy spells to try to drive them out. Here is one, should you wish to use it, which they claim is an excellent rite for the purpose: 'I conjure you, demon, whoever you are, by this god, SABARBARBATHIOTH SABARBARBA-THIOUTH SABARBARBATHIONETH SABAR-BARBAPHAI – Come out, demon, whoever you are, and stay away from him.'

Mental distress is best avoided by living and working in an environment conducive to well-being. Live in a house that is light, airy in summer, but sunny in winter. Keep out of the midday sun and avoid the evening chill. Try not to breathe in the vapours from rivers and marshes since these can provoke pestilence. Do not devote all your time to affairs of business, which leaves you little time for the care of your body. Those that do so are no better than voluntary slaves. The baths are an excellent way to remove stress. If you dream of washing in baths that are beautiful, bright and moderately heated it is auspicious, for it signifies wealth and success in business for the healthy, and health for the sick. The baths are also good for cleaning out a fresh wound or ulcer. But do not overindulge. The continued use of baths undermines a man's strength and weakens the muscle of the body in the same way that boiling tenderises meat. Still, as the saying goes: 'Baths, wine and women ruin our bodies – but they make life worth living!'

Arrange your life around the seasons of the year. In

winter it is right to eat more and to drink a stronger wine. Bread, meat – preferably boiled – and some vegetables will all help promote heat within the body. In spring, your intake of food must be reduced and your wine should be watered down. More meat should be eaten, especially roast meat. Game is best eaten then. In summer, the body needs more food and drink to give it energy to work. It is in autumn that the greatest danger lies. The changes in the weather can easily destabilise your body. So do not go outdoors unless well covered and wearing stout shoes. Do not sleep outside. Some believe that fruit is harmful, and if eaten immoderately this may be true.

Make sure that you get the right amount of sleep. If your constitution is weak – as is the case with most city-dwellers and almost all those who enjoy literature – you should only get up early if you have digested well from the previous evening. If not, you must stay in bed or, if you have been obliged to get up early, go back to bed later and sleep some more. If you have failed to digest, stay in bed all day, without working or exercising or attending to any business matters. On waking up, you should always lie still for a while then bathe the face with cold water. Take a siesta during the summer before lunch. In winter, it is best to stay in bed throughout the hours of darkness. If you must work by lamplight, give yourself time to digest your dinner first.

If you find it difficult to get up in the morning, remind yourself that you are a human being and that this is what you are meant to do. You are simply doing the work of a human. Before going to sleep at night, you should think about everything you have done during the day and ask how you have made yourself a better person. What bad habits have you cured yourself of? There is no better sleep than that following self-examination. How deep and calm is the sleep of a mind at peace with itself. This is something I do every night. When the torch has been removed by the slave and my wife is asleep, I examine my entire day and measure how well I have done, without any favouritism to myself, nor indeed any hostility.

Health is harmony. Everything must be done in moderation to maintain the balance of your body. Nothing must be done in excess. Do not eat too much or too little, just enough to nourish the body and be digested well. And if you do overdo one thing – whether it is food, the baths, sex or wine – make sure that you correct the fault. The best way to correct excess is opposite excess: so rest cures overwork, abstention relieves the hangover and so on. Nature knows how to stay healthy, but it is up to us to help nature in whatever way we can. Living in this way is a life skill we can all learn. We can all be healthy at every stage of our life.

If you wish to change your habits you should do so gradually. If you lie about doing nothing for a long time and then have to work hard you will find it a shock. If you find yourself having to do a lot of physical work when you are unused to it, you should afterwards go to bed on an empty stomach, especially if you have a bitter taste in your mouth or your bowels are disturbed. Before eating, you should take a gentle walk and sit in the warm baths and be anointed with oil. If you have become overheated from being in the sun when you are not used to it, you should go at once to the baths and there have oil poured over your head and body. Then enter a hot tub and have a slave pour plenty of water over your head. If you have to travel by sea and find that it makes you sick, you should eat nothing. Only if you have spewed up sour phlegm should you eat something, but keep it lighter than usual. If you feel nauseous during the voyage but are not actually sick, either eat nothing or make yourself vomit after food.

It is far easier to maintain health than to cure illness. If you do fall sick, however, let me guide you through various treatments you will find useful and efficacious. If you suffer from stomach pains, read to yourself out loud, then take a walk and exercise at handball or at something that works the upper parts of the body. Next, drink hot wine through a thin tube on an empty stomach and restrict yourself to two light meals a day. Weakness of the stomach is indicated by pallor, wasting, pain over the heart and involuntary vomiting. If you display none of these symptoms, your stomach is sound.

If your sinews and ligaments are painful, exercise the affected part as much as possible. You should even expose it to hard work or to cold, unless the pain is growing worse, in which case rest and fresh air is the best cure. Eating game is the worst thing you can do as it impedes the digestion, which is most harmful to any part of the body that is injured.

You should learn to understand your own body's particular weaknesses. Just as digestion affects all differently, so does heat or cold. In general, heat is bad for the elderly and for the thin, for those who have been wounded, and for those with afflictions of the lower bodily regions, such as the bladder, womb and genitals. Cold makes the skin turn pale, grey and hard. But in the young, cold is beneficial as it is to fat people. Cold also keeps the mind more vigorous and sharpens up the digestion. Heat, by contrast, benefits all that cold harms. It gives the skin a good colour and promotes urination. If extreme, heat weakens the body by softening the sinews and relaxing the stomach. It can also prevent sleep, generate exhaustion through excessive sweating and leave the body vulnerable to pestilence.

If a plague strikes the area where you live you should take the following precautions. If possible, go abroad. If you cannot do this, have your slaves carry you about in a litter, or walk outside only before the hottest part of the day. Avoid becoming fatigued and do not eat so much as to provoke indigestion. Do not get up early in the morning or walk about in your bare feet, especially after a meal or bath. Do not make yourself vomit at any time nor take any laxatives. It is far better for your bowels to be restrained than be too loose. Alternate between drinking water one day and wine the next. If you take these precautions you will keep healthy during attacks of pestilence, particularly those brought in by southerly winds. You will also find this advice useful if you are travelling during an unhealthy part of the year or are passing through an unhealthy region.

You may well find at some time or other that you are bitten by a poisonous spider or snake. One famous doctor, called Mithridates, experimented with using herbs against such poisons by giving them to condemned criminals. He found that some were very useful against scorpion stings, and others against poisonous plants, such as aconite. So he mixed them all together to make a single super drug that he hoped could be used against all poisons. Some years later, the emperor Nero's head physician, Andromachus, added to this a considerable amount of dried snake flesh and so invented what is known as the Theriac antidote. If you fear that you are a target for assassination, you can take a small dose of the drug daily as a preventative against being poisoned. If you need the compound after having been bitten or poisoned, then you will have to take four or five times as much to counteract it.

Bites are a common affliction, whether from a dog, ape or wild animal. Almost every bite has within it a poison of some sort. If the wound is severe, put a cup over it immediately but if it is only slight then cover it with a paste, so long as it is not greasy. Salt is a good remedy for bites, especially those from a dog. Place a hand over the bite and strike the back of it with two fingers of the other hand. This draws out the pus from the wound. If the dog was mad, the poison must be drawn out by a cup. Provided the wound is not among sinews and muscles, it should be cauterised. If that is not possible, the victim should be bled. After the bite of a mad dog, some doctors recommend that the patient goes to the baths at once and spends as long as they can in the hottest room in order to sweat out the poison. Then they say that the victim should pour wine over the wound since wine is an antidote to all poisons. When this has been done for three days, the patient is deemed to be out of danger.

The gods will often warn you in your dreams about impending illness and what its end result will be. One man I know dreamt that a javelin fell from the sky and wounded him in one of his feet. The next day he was bitten in the same foot by a snake, gangrene set in and he died. In another dream I heard about, a man dreamt that the god Asclepius wounded him in the belly with a sword and he died. The man did indeed develop an abscess in his belly but he was cured after undergoing surgery, for Asclepius is the god of healing and the sword signified that he would successfully be operated upon. In another dream I read about, a man who was sick went into the temple of Zeus and asked the god whether he would survive or not. Zeus said nothing but nodded affirmatively with his head. Naturally, the man died the next day. This should not surprise you for by nodding his head downwards the god looked to the earth where the dead are buried.

As an aside, may I warn you that you will find your household slaves will often claim to be sick. It is important for you to know how to detect malingerers. Some will create a swelling by deliberately applying a drug to their bodies. Others will spit blood at the end of a bout of coughing by biting on a gum and making it bleed. Or they will pretend to be insane. I once heard of a man who was summoned by the town's citizens to appear before the assembly and pretended to have severe colic so he didn't have to appear. A doctor who was at the scene ordered hot poultices to be applied to him but the man didn't seem to want any help. And, of course, the moment the assembly finished he stopped shrieking and wailing as if in pain. It did not take a doctor to work out he was faking it.

I remember also a slave of mine who claimed he was suffering extreme pain in his knee. He was one of those slaves who run alongside their masters in the streets. It was noticeable that the pain increased whenever I was about to go anywhere far away. I also found out from one of his fellow slaves that the young man was in love with one of the slave girls and wanted to stay with her while I was away. He had even applied some mustard to the knee to produce a slight swelling. In any case he hadn't done anything to hurt his knee and refused any treatment. Nor could he really describe the pain in any detail, whether it was spread wide and felt numb and heavy, or was stabbing and throbbing or felt like it was pulling the flesh apart. Those who are really in pain generally don't show much distress. And if they are in agony they will accept any treatment no matter how severe. If they are malingering, they are afraid of any treatment no matter how innocuous.

Most of the medical advice I have given you so far is drawn from my knowledge of Greek doctors. There is a problem with using such doctors: they are expensive. They are also often contradictory in their diagnoses. In any case, why should we believe those who are out to make money from saving lives? Medicine is the only profession where any man off the street gains our immediate trust if he calls himself a doctor. We are lulled by the sweet hope of being healed when it is often not clear that these people know what they are doing. We risk our lives for their benefit and if they happen to kill a man they suffer no penalty for it. So if you prefer your cures to be traditional and homespun – and a good bit cheaper – then you should refer to the following remedies.

If you are unlucky enough to break a bone, cover it with the ashes of the jawbone of a pig. Or boil some lard and pack it around the break: this will mend it amazingly quickly. In my experience, broken ribs are best treated with a compress of goat's manure mixed with wine. Have the slaves on your country estates collect pig manure in springtime and dry it. You can then boil it in vinegar to produce an excellent treatment for bruises, which is effective even on charioteers who have been run over. The powder is best drunk mixed with water and they say that the emperor Nero used to refresh himself with this drink because he wanted to prove to professional charioteers that he was one of them.

For epilepsy, it is beneficial to eat a bear's testes or those of a wild boar mixed in mare's milk. Wild-boar urine in honey works well, especially if it has first been allowed to dry out in the dead animal's bladder. Or try eating the lungs of a hare that have been preserved in salt, to which has been added frankincense and wine. Other remedies include smoked ass's brain in honey. If you feel the onset of a fit, breathe in the smell from the afterbirth of a donkey that has given birth to a male foal. This will repel the seizure. There are some who recommend eating the heart of a black jackass on the first or second day of the moon or prescribe drinking its blood mixed with vinegar for forty days. To treat mental delirium, you can mix an ass's urine with water from a blacksmith's, in which hot iron has been dipped. Yet another remedy for epilepsy is for the patient to stand upright and drink a draught made from the suet fat of a goat that has been boiled in an equal measure of bull's gall.

A remedy for melancholia is calf's dung that has been boiled in wine. Victims of lethargy can be energised by smelling the fumes from burnt goat's horns or wild boar's liver. Consumptives benefit by eating wolf's liver in thin wine, by the lard of a sow fed on herbs, and also by donkey meat served in gravy. The smoke from the dried dung of an ox that has been fed on green fodder, inhaled through a reed, is also said to be beneficial. Some authorities hold that consumptive coughs are also cured by eating the suet of a she-goat in porridge or the lung of a stag that has been smoked and then ground up with wine.

Dislocated joints are best treated with the fresh dung of a wild boar or an application of beef. Swellings can be reduced by applying pig manure that has been warmed in an earthenware pot and mixed with oil. Any hardened mass on the body can be removed by an application of wolf fat. Sores are best treated with ox dung warmed on hot cinders, boils with salted beef suet. Grease burns with bear fat mixed with the roots of lilies or the ash of burnt pig bristles combined with pig fat. If you wish to avoid having a scar, then also use the manure of a she-goat. The best quality glue is made from the ears and genitals of bulls and this also acts as an excellent remedy for burns. Cat faeces will help you remove thorns from your skin as will the rennet of a hare mixed with powdered frankincense and oil or mistletoe and bee glue.

A woman is the only animal that has monthly periods.

She alone therefore has what are called moles in her womb. These moles are shapeless masses of flesh that move about and can stop menstruation and even childbirth from occurring. They can also cause death in the woman, sometimes when the bowels are moving in a violent fashion. A woman's periods can be helped by applying the gall of a bull with unwashed wool. Nothing in nature can be found which is more remarkable than the monthly flux of women. If the emission comes into contact with new wine, it will turn it sour. Crops touched by it wither and die, seeds in the garden shrivel, and the fruit of trees falls off. If a shiny mirror even so much as reflects it, then the surface is dimmed. Knives are blunted by it, whole beehives are killed by it, and contact will make bronze and iron rust instantly. The taste of it will drive dogs mad and infects their bites with an incurable poison.

Problems with the womb are best treated by fumigating the uterus with deer's hair. I have also heard it reported that female deer swallow a stone when they realise they are pregnant. If this is recovered and worn as an amulet, it will prevent miscarriage. Pains in the uterus are relieved by eating wolf liver, while the flesh is beneficial for women who are about to give birth. Hare is also very good for pregnant women. Its lung should be dried and taken in liquid form to ease delivery, while the rennet helps ease the passage of the afterbirth, especially if mixed with saffron and leek juice. Inserting a block of this into the vagina will also draw out a dead foetus.

If your wife is pregnant and you want her to have a boy, get her to eat a hare's womb mixed into her food. Or have her eat the animal's testicles. Similarly, having your wife eat roast veal with the plant aristolochia at about the time of conception ensures a male child. If your wife is into her thirties and so almost past childbearing age, feeding her the foetus of a hare, taken fresh from its womb, will generate renewed fertility in her. Hare is also useful in that eating nine pellets of its droppings will make a young woman's breasts permanently firm.

Childbirth can be eased by drinking sow's milk with honey wine. A feeding mother's breasts will swell less if rubbed with a sow's blood; and if her nipples are painful, they can be soothed by drinking ass's milk. If the womb suffers any ulcerations, these can be healed by the application in unprocessed wool of the dried suet of a sow, while a prolapse of the uterus can be contained by an injection of butter. A mother's milk supply can be made plentiful by rubbing the dried spleen of a donkey on to the breasts. Childbirth pangs can easily result in future sterility. Such barrenness can be cured by rubbing a mixture of snake fat, copper rust and honey on to the genitals before intercourse.

Here are some other ways of preventing pregnancy, in addition to those I mentioned earlier. Midwives assure us that a woman's periods, however full, can be stopped by drinking the urine of a she-goat or by applying its dung to the vagina. Some say that if the loins of a woman are rubbed thoroughly with the blood of a tick from a black wild-bull, she will be disgusted by the very idea of sexual intercourse. Or if you get her to drink the urine of a he-goat – use nard to disguise the foul taste – this will put her off having sex with you entirely and so prevent her from becoming pregnant.

An alternative to both Greek medicine and these traditional remedies is to pay a visit to the healing god Asclepius. His temples are very popular and you will easily find one near you. Note that it is normal practice, after you have made offerings to the god, to sleep within the temple precinct. The god can then be expected to call on you in your sleep and either cure you or communicate to you in a dream what treatments you should undertake. People often write short accounts of their illnesses and their divinely inspired cures on the walls outside the temple. I remember one which read, 'A man who had his toe healed by a serpent. He was taken outside by the temple servants with a malignant sore on his toe and sat upon a seat. While he slept the god disguised as a snake crawled out of the shrine and licked his toe. The patient woke up and was healed. He said that in a dream he had seen a beautiful youth put a drug on his toe.'

I visited a temple of Asclepius once. I had to bathe regularly. I dreamt my food had not digested properly. I consulted the priest who suggested I vomit in the evening. Next night, the god ordered me to do many strange things. So when the harbour waves were swollen by the south wind and ships were in distress, I had to row across to the opposite side, while eating honey and acorns, and then vomit. The following day I was commanded to bathe in snow, an order I gladly obeyed, since it soon brought about a cure and my pain ended.

There is one more source of treatment. Magic. This is not simple superstition, such as the widespread belief that cutting your hair on either the seventeenth or nineteenth day of the month prevents baldness and headaches. It is the use of supernatural powers to bring about cures and prevent other spirits from attacking you. Naturally, I do not believe in it, but I tell you here in case you do. In its simplest form, you can wear amulets to ward off evil forces. Gaius Licinius Mucianus, for example, the three times consul, used to put a living fly in a small piece of linen cloth and tie it round his neck, claiming that this kept him free of eye inflammation. More complicated spells can be used to cure more serious complaints. Any kind of dislocation, they say, may be cured by the following charm. Take a green reed four or five feet long and split it down the middle, and let two men hold it to your hips. Begin to chant, 'motas uaeta daries dardares astataries dissunapiter' and continue until the pieces of reed meet. Brandish a knife over these pieces and the dislocation or fracture will heal. Other well-known magical cures include the following. For toothache, put your hands behind your back and bite off a piece of wood that has been struck by lightning and apply it to the tooth. To cure someone suffering a fever, take a nail that has been used to crucify a criminal or runaway slave and wrap it in wool and tie it round the patient's neck. For a headache, write ABRASAX on scarlet parchment, make it into a plaster and then place it on the side of the head. But, whether you believe in it or not, you may wish to protect yourself against others trying to make you ill by using magic against you, just in case. Wear an amulet which has been made in the following way: take a triangular piece of pot from a crossroads in your left hand and write on it with ink mixed with myrrh

'ASTRAELOS CHRAELOS – ruin every spell that is cast against me [insert your own name here] because I pray by your great and terrifying names, names which the very winds shudder at, names which the very sound of can shatter rocks.'

·· COMMENTARY ··

We in the western world have access to a medical system that supplies all kinds of extraordinary treatments. People in antiquity worried about their health just as much as we do today but their ability to treat illness was limited and so far more emphasis was placed on maintaining one's health in the first place. They also had very different ways of understanding health and illness.

Medical writings ranged from the early works attributed to Hippocrates of Cos, who died around 375 BC, to those of later writers under the Roman empire, such as Aretaeus, Caelius Aurelianus, Celsus and, above all, Galen, who served as the Roman emperor Marcus Aurelius's personal physician and is known to have written more than 350 works. Most medical theorists believed that the body contained four humours – named in the most influential text of humoral medicine, Hippocrates's *On the Nature of Man*, as black bile, yellow bile, blood and phlegm. These theories suggested that the types of illness a patient suffered reflected different levels of heat and moisture within the body, which affected the balance of these four liquids. But beyond this, these medical writers agreed about little. They worked in a competitive marketplace and had to attract customers to their own particular kinds of treatment. Each doctor had his own approach to disease and healing, and even though these are often grouped together as 'schools', in reality they did not represent formal divisions but broadly similar approaches to medicine. Doctors known, somewhat confusingly, as Methodists, argued that all diseases could be categorised by a simple method of diagnosis: those caused by constriction, by relaxation or by a mixture of the two. The Empiricists rejected such universal theories. They thought it was best to treat the particular symptoms of the individual patient. The Rationalists believed it was necessary to look beyond superficial symptoms to try to understand the underlying causes of disease.

This kind of medical theory was a Greek import and many Romans distrusted it for that reason. Pliny the Elder's *Natural History*, for example, contains copious information about treatments that can be carried out within the home by the head of the household, especially in Books 28–9. The treatments make use of the kind of things you would find easily on the average Roman estate, such as dung and common animal parts. This meant that there was no need to bring in one of those dodgy Greek doctors at all.

The *Sacred Tales* of Aelius Aristides give a fascinating glimpse into the mindset of a devoted follower of Asclepius. He maintained a journal for decades, which recorded in the minutest detail all the dreams, physical ailments and treatments the god sent to him. With its endless attention to the smallest changes in his physical condition, he comes across as more neurotic than the most extreme modern hypochondriac. It is easy to imagine that receiving the detailed attention of the temple priests and attendants within a healing context delivered a placebo effect that may well have been powerful enough to cause an improvement in many cases.

There was no simple divide between medical treatments, traditional remedies and religious treatments. Physicians worked at the temples of Asclepius. Nor was there any straightforward opposition between medicine and faith-based healing. Galen himself trained as a doctor following a dream in which Asclepius appeared to his father, and later used the god to avoid going on campaign with the imperial household to Germany by claiming, somewhat conveniently, that he had been told by Asclepius in a dream not to travel.

The bulk of this chapter has been based on various works by Galen and Celsus's *On Medicine*. Seneca's *Letters* 18 outlines the benefits of fasting. Vegetius (*On Military Matters* 1) describes the kind of training a new recruit to the Roman army would undergo. His description of carrying a rucksack weighing 60 lbs equates to a modern 20 kg or 44 lbs. On ancient attitudes and treatments regarding mental health, see the second chapter of my *Popular Culture in Ancient Rome*. The account of the self-harming starving man can be found in John Chrysostom *Sermon on the First Letter to the Corinthians* 21.5–6 (*Patrologia Graeca* 61.177–8). The New Testament (Luke 8:26–9) describes the sad fate of the Gerasene demoniac who lived alone on the edge of town. The *Greek Magical Papyri*

(4.1227–64) has a spell to exorcise demons. Magic being used to treat illness can be found in Cato's *On Agriculture* 160, Pliny the Elder *Natural History* 28.11.45–6 and the *Greek Magical Papyri* (7.201–2; 36.256–64). Dreams relating to illness can be found in Artemidorus's *Interpretation of Dreams* (e.g. 5.59, 5.61, 5.71).

CHAPTER VIII

THE GODS HELP THOSE THAT HELP THEM

WHAT IS IT THAT MAKES us Romans so successful? To be sure, it is our moral courage, our drive to conquer, our ability to run our households properly. But ultimately all this would count for nothing if we did not also have the support of the gods. If you are to enjoy success on a Roman scale, you too will have to learn how to get, and keep, the gods on your side. Let me tell you how to approach the powers of the pantheon, how to interpret what they are telling you, and how to use them to help you crush your enemies.

What do you say to a god? What can you, a weak human being, do to make them deign to notice your call for help and then bother to respond to it? Your simple statement is this: 'I give you something so that you will give me something.' This is the message which you must reinforce continually through your actions: that you make sacrifice and offer the gods a variety of offerings – whether prayers, vows or sacrifices – in the belief that these will please them and encourage them to intervene on your behalf. To be sure, the gods will not always listen to you or be influenced by your gifts. But if you maintain a consistent pattern of appropriate piety they will, in the long run, grant you their favour in return. It is this mutually beneficial relationship between the weak and the powerful that is the driving force, not just of life on earth, but of the very universe itself.

It does no good to offer sacrifice or consult the gods without using both the correct ceremonies and the right words for the particular occasion. Some words are appropriate for seeking favourable omens, others for getting help, others still for warding off misfortune. In our law courts, for example, you hear set prayers being read out loud by an attendant, which he recites verbatim from a book to ensure that nothing is said out of turn, while another attendant checks that the formula is being read correctly. Another makes sure that everyone maintains a respectful silence and a flute player performs so that any noise from outside does not interrupt the proceedings.

Performing the proper prayers is vital on your estates. Before you harvest spelt, wheat, beans or barley, you should sacrifice a pig to the god of crops, Ceres. Offer votive cakes to Janus with the following words: 'Father Janus, in offering you these cakes and wine, I humbly beg you to be merciful to me and my children, my house and my household.' Next you must make another cake offering to Jupiter, repeating the words. Then remove the entrails of the pig and offer them to the gods along with another votive cake and more libations of wine.

If you wish to thin out a grove of trees, you must sacrifice a pig with the following prayer: 'Whatever god has had this grove dedicated to him, it is his right to receive a sacrifice in return for the benefit we receive from thinning it. In offering this pig, I humbly beg you to be merciful to me and my children, my house and my household. Please accept this pig which I offer.' Before ploughing the land, you should offer a sacrifice in the same way but add the words 'for the sake of doing this work'. This ritual must be performed on every day the ploughing continues. If you miss a day, or a public holiday intervenes, a new offering must be made. This is the formula for purifying newly cultivated land. Lead about a pig, sheep and bull, which are to be your sacrificial offerings, then say, 'May the help of the gods bring success to our work and purify my farm, my land and my ground with this sacrifice.' Pray and offer wine to Janus and Jupiter, using the same formula as above, adding some words to Mars: 'Father Mars, I beseech you to ward off sickness, barrenness and destruction from my fields, but permit my crops to flourish and bring forth rich harvests.' When you kill the sacrificial animals, recite the formula: 'With this blow, deign to accept this offering.' Inspect the entrails, and if favourable omens are not obtained because the livers are unclean, speak as follows: 'Father Mars, if anything has displeased you with these offerings, I make atonement with new victims,' and repeat the sacrifice with new animals until the desired outcome is achieved. If just one of the animals' entrails has disappointed then you need only repeat the sacrifice with another animal of that type.

Many festivals must also be properly observed. In the Robigalia, you must reach a peace with Robigus, the god of mildew (although some say it is a goddess). This happens, naturally enough, during April when the god makes his presence most commonly felt. Sacrifice a dog and offer its entrails and those of a sheep to the flames, with the words, 'Scaly Mildew, spare our blades of corn and let their tender tips quiver above the earth.' Then pour incense and wine on to the burning guts.

And then there is the festival of the Lupercalia – the feast of the wolves – that takes place in February. I have no idea why the festival bears such a name. Rome obviously owes a great debt to the she-wolf that suckled our illustrious founder Romulus and his ill-fated brother Remus. It is certainly the case that the wolf-priests, as they are known, start their run round the city from the point where Romulus is said to have been abandoned as a baby. But the festivities that follow are hard to fathom. The wolf-priests slaughter a dog and some goats, then two young noblemen are smeared with the blood on their foreheads, which is then immediately wiped off with milk-soaked wool. The youths must laugh once they have been so cleaned. Then they cut the goat skins into strips and run through the city, naked, hitting everyone they meet with them. No one tries to get out of their way. In fact, young newly married women actively get in their way because it is commonly believed that being struck results in pregnancy and an easy birth.

There are as many rituals as there are activities. You must learn the correct form of approach to the gods according to what it is you are trying to achieve. As for the gods themselves, they are as numerous as the stars – their names could fill ten volumes – and you must focus your attention on the correct deity. In the countryside, for example, farms are dedicated to Rusina, the mountains to Jugatinus, the downs are looked over by the goddess Collatina, and the valleys by Vallonia. When it comes to your crops, Seia protects the seed corn before it sprouts, Segetia when it is grown above. Proserpina is the goddess set over the germinating seeds, Nodotus over the knots of the stems, and Voluntina protects the sheaths that hold the ears of corn. The goddess Matuta looks over the process of ripening, and Flora the time when the grain comes into flower. Once the grain is harvested and stored, the goddess Tutilina keeps it safe. When the crop is finally pulled from the earth, it is the goddess Runcina to which this job is ascribed. And there are others besides. If you are to perform the correct ritual to the right deity in the correct fashion at the right time, you have to pay attention to all these details. Even the entrance to your house has three gods assigned to its functions. The doors belong to Forculus, the hinges to Cardea and the threshold to Limentinus.

The high priest of our religion, the Pontifex Maximus, holds the greatest power. Originally, his duties included maintaining the wooden bridge across the Tiber, from which he drew the title 'Supreme Bridge-builder'. But he and his fellow priests are in charge of far more important matters than that. For it is their job to ensure that bridges are maintained, as it were, between men and gods. They serve as judges in all religious disputes between the Romans, whether citizens or magistrates. It is they who decide the laws regarding the observance of religious rites. It is they who investigate whether magistrates and priests have carried out their religious duties properly, and ensure that religious rites are carried out in accordance with sacred law. They interpret all matters relating to the worship of the gods and if anyone should dare to disobey their religious orders, the priests can punish them in accordance with the severity of the offence. In matters of religion, they themselves are not liable to either prosecution or punishment, nor are they accountable to the senate or the Roman people.

These most holy Roman men are also responsible for choosing the most holy Roman women – the six Vestal Virgins. If you wish for one of your daughters to aspire to this great honour you should be aware of the following selection criteria. The girl must be taken when she is between six and ten years of age. Both of her parents must still be alive at this point. She must also be free from any speech impediment or hearing impairment, and must have no other physical defects. Neither parent can ever have been a slave or have worked in any degrading occupation, such as that of butcher, fishmonger, actor or the like. The girl's father must also be resident in Italy.

Traditionally, twenty prospective candidates are selected from the people at the discretion of the Pontifex Maximus. The final selection is then carried out by lot. But these days this is hardly ever necessary. If any father of respectable birth offers his daughter to the Pontifex Maximus, and provided that her candidacy does not violate any religious law, then the priest is permitted to accept her. The honour associated with the position means that a steady supply of candidates is generally forthcoming, without the need to resort to choosing girls by random selection.

As soon as the young Vestal is chosen she is escorted to the House of Vesta, which is located on the edge of the Roman forum, next to the Palatine hill, where she is handed over to the Pontiff. He symbolically grabs her hand and drags her away from her father as if she had been captured in war. At this point she passes from the control of her father and acquires the right to make a will. The Pontiff then says to her, 'I take you as one who has fulfilled all the legal requirements to be a priestess of Vesta for you to perform all the rites it is legal for a Vestal to perform for the benefit of the Roman people.' The Vestals live in the temple of the goddess and anyone is allowed to go in and see them during the daytime. But at night, no man may enter the building. The Vestals are required to remain undefiled by marriage for thirty years, instead devoting themselves to offering sacrifices and performing the other rites laid down by holy law. During the first ten years, they learn their various functions, in the second ten years they perform them, and during the final decade they pass on their knowledge to the newcomers. At the end of their thirty-year term, they are free to marry once they have put aside the hair bands and other insignia of their office. A few have indeed got married, but they have all come to such dreadful ends that most see this as divine retribution from the goddess for abandoning her and so they remain as virgins in the temple until they die.

The great glory that goes with the post means that most Vestals feel no desire to marry or have children. The severest punishments await those who fall short of the high standards the position demands. The pontiffs themselves investigate any allegations of misconduct and carry out the punishment. For lesser misdemeanours, the Vestals are beaten with rods. But those who abandon the second half of their title are delivered up to suffer the most shameful and miserable death. While still alive, they are dressed in funeral attire and carried on a bier as part of a solemn funeral procession. All their family and friends walk beside them, weeping in lamentation. At the Colline Gate, they reach an underground cell. The small vault contains a couch, a lamp and a table with a little food. The Pontifex Maximus raises his hands to the heavens and utters a prayer before he leads the condemned Vestal to the common executioner, who directs her to the ladder leading down into the cell. Once she has descended, the ladder is drawn up, the pit is filled with earth until the surface is level with the surrounding ground and she is left to perish.

I once had the misfortune of seeing the senior Vestal punished in this way on the orders of the emperor. Many of us were convinced she was innocent of the charges of unchastity laid against her and the way she went to her death only confirmed those doubts. She did everything she could to keep her dignity intact as she went down into the chamber. At one point her robe caught on the ladder and she turned to gather it up. When the executioner offered her his hand she recoiled from it in disgust, spurning contact with such a foul individual when she was, in fact, still pure, chaste and holy. With graceful deportment she lowered herself down into her living tomb and died with probity and decorum.

You might wonder how unfaithful Vestals are discovered. Often the goddess herself sends a sign by extinguishing the sacred eternal flame that burns in her temple. The Romans dread this more than anything, since they see it as an omen portending the destruction of the city. Once the offending Vestal has been dealt with in the manner described, fire is again brought into the temple with many supplicatory rites to appease the offended goddess and restore good order.

The reason the state takes these matters so seriously is simple: the gods will only support the Romans to the degree to which they please them. It therefore follows that the more they please their divine masters, the more successful the Romans will be. We owe our domination of the world to our pious worship of the gods and we will only maintain our position of power if the gods continue to wish it so.

The gods are actively involved in all Roman conquests. Before we fought King Antiochus of Syria, for example, the senate promised great gifts to Jupiter if the gods should grant us victory. The vow was made through the Pontifex Maximus, who pronounced the following formula: 'If the war which the Roman people has ordered to be waged against King Antiochus be successful, then they shall celebrate in your honour, Jupiter, Great Games for the space of ten days, and large gifts of money shall be made to all your shrines.' When we advance against an enemy town, the army's priests recite another formula that aims to win the enemy's gods over to our side by making clear to them that their statues will be treated with care during the sacking of the city and that they will continue to be worshipped afterwards. How much more appealing to a god to be worshipped by the powerful Romans than to remain the object of devotion of a weak and failing state. 'Whether you are a god or a goddess,' they call out, 'who hold under your protection the people of this city, I pray to you and respectfully implore you that you abandon this people and city and desert their buildings, temples and houses, and fill the people with fear and terror. Come over to Rome! Our city and temples will be far more agreeable to you and we Romans will look after you so well that you will appreciate the difference. If you do this, I vow that we will build you temples and celebrate games in your honour.'

Omens are taken before battle commences. Before we defeated the Samnites, for example, the troops were so confident of victory and of having the favour of heaven that they were clamouring to be led into battle. But the consul who was commanding the army knew how important it was to test the level of the gods' support. He ordered the priest to observe the omens and they fed the sacred corn to the holy chickens. Caught up in the universal excitement that filled the Roman troops, the priest could not believe it when the chickens refused to eat up their feed. He therefore reported that the chickens had eaten so greedily that the corn fell from their mouths. Delighted with the news, the consul spread the news that the omens could not be more favourable and ordered preparations for battle to commence.

Some cavalrymen had seen the omens take place and told the consul what had really happened. But he told them not to worry. 'If the man who is taking the omens makes a false report,' he said, 'he will bring down divine wrath on his own head. As far as I am concerned, I have received the formal advice that the chickens ate eagerly and there could be no more favourable omen for the Roman army.' He then ordered the priest to fight in the front rank of the troops and gave the signal for the battle to commence. At that very moment, a crow landed in front of him and gave a loud and distinct call. The commander welcomed the good omen and declared that the gods had never given a clearer signal of their support for Rome. He then ordered the charge to be sounded and the battle shout to be raised. Sure enough, the Samnites were crushed but the deceitful priest was mortally wounded in the fray.

The gods cannot be ignored. Claudius Pulcher once began a sea battle off Sicily even though the sacred chickens would not eat when he took the auspices. In anger, he threw them into the sea, saying that if they would not eat then they would drink. He was defeated. And sometimes the news the omens convey has a bitter edge. Before leading the armies out to battle near Mount Vesuvius, the consul Decius offered sacrifice. The priest inspected the victim's organs and found them favourable apart from a clear sign that the commander himself would die. 'So be it,' Decius simply replied and marched to both certain victory and certain death.

The gods conferred one particularly good piece of fortune on Rome long ago when the kings still ruled, which has saved it from all kinds of disaster and benefits it still to this day. One day an unknown foreign woman called Sibyl came up to King Tarquin and offered him nine books filled with prophecies. When Tarquin refused to buy the books, she went away and burned three of them. Soon after, she returned and offered him the remaining six books for the same price. The king thought she was a fool and sent her away again, at which point she burned another three. Once again she soon returned, now offering only three books for the same price. The king started to wonder what was going on and sent for the priests. They immediately recognised certain signs that revealed these books to be a blessing from the gods and told the king to pay up for the remaining three. He did so and the woman bade him to take great care of them before disappearing, never to be seen again. Tarquin chose two distinguished men to guard the books with the help of two slaves. So seriously did the king take this matter that when he was told that one of the men, Marcus Atilius, was not taking his job seriously he had him punished as if he had killed his own father by having him sewn up in a leather bag together with a dog, a cock, a viper and an ape and thrown into the sea. Ever since then, the Roman state has looked after these Sibylline books with great care, more than they give to any other possession. By order of the senate the books are consulted whenever the state is in the grip of strife or when some great misfortune has happened in war, or some important portents have been seen which are difficult to interpret, as is often the case. Then, during the war against our allies, disaster struck and the temple in which the books were kept was burned down, itself a sure sign of the gods' disapproval of this civil war. Only scraps remain of the originals, and parts that had been copied from them, but they still provide the best advice the state can ever obtain.

One such nugget came during the second war against Carthage and its great general, Hannibal. Dire portents seemed to threaten Rome's imminent demise: a shower of meteors lit up the sky, the harvests failed and famine ensued. In this dreadful situation, the senate called for the Sibylline books to be consulted and interpreted their message as saying that Rome would be defeated unless it imported the cult of the Great Mother from Asia. The home of this goddess was at that time in the kingdom of Pergamum, an ally of Rome, and ambassadors were sent to negotiate a transfer. Soon after, the goddess arrived in the port of Ostia. Rome's best man, Cornelius Scipio, was sent to meet the statue of the goddess and, along with the city's most virtuous women, conducted her to the Temple of Victory to await the completion of her own splendid temple on the Palatine hill. All the Roman citizens flocked to greet the new goddess, holding censers containing burning incense and uttering earnest prayers as she passed by them in the street.

It was later discovered that the Great Mother had originally been a Trojan goddess and therefore had been worshipped by Aeneas, who first brought the Roman people to Italy when he fled Troy after its destruction. The goddess was simply coming home, as it were. But, all the same, she brought with her a few surprises. Her priests, the Cocks, on the Day of Blood, process with her through the streets – yellow-robed, banging drums and cymbals, blasting horns and flutes, whipping themselves until they bleed and finally, in an ecstatic frenzy, castrating themselves. Each priest then throws his severed manhood through the open windows of the houses they pass. Since this seemed excessive behaviour by Roman standards, only a few were permitted to adopt this practice and instead those wishing to be initiated in the mysteries may offer a bloody animal sacrifice in its place. In the Criobolium you offer a ram, while in the Taurobolium you sacrifice a bull. My brother once took part in this rite and naturally offered a bull since this is by far the most costly option. He stood in a pit beneath a grate, on which stood the animal. The throat was cut and the bull's blood poured through the grate on to his initiate head beneath, and he emerged to the audience's applause drenched in the bright red gore.

The gods speak to you in many ways. The ways in which the birds fly, the movements of the constellations, the arrangement of the features of your hand or face, moles on your body or the way limbs twitch can all reveal what the gods have in store for you and tell you how you should act. And there are many other media besides: dreams, dishes, cheese, sieves, and summoning the spirits of the dead can all be interpreted so that you can understand their hidden message. Naturally, you will need to consult experts in such matters but these can easily be found in most marketplaces. You should consult with these diviners on all kinds of issues. I myself have asked for all sorts of advice concerning such things as locating runaway slaves, freeing slaves, buying land, building new houses, pregnancy, marriage for relatives, leaving money in my will, illness and travel.

In case you wonder what it is like to consult an oracle, let me describe a trip I once made to a diviner near the lake of Avernus. I entered a dark cave, which was famous for being a place where it was possible to call up the dead. I had first to repeat the sacred formula, offer a libation of wine and sacrifice several animals. I called upon the spirit of my dead father, whose advice I was seeking. Then he appeared, an insubstantial shade, difficult both to see and to recognise, yet endowed with a human voice and form. He answered the questions I put to him and then vanished.

Beware of charlatans. A friend of mine once visited an incompetent astrologer because his son was sick. The astrologer cast the boy's horoscope and said, 'Fear not, he will be a lawyer, then a city-official, then a governor.' Two days later the child died. His father confronted the astrologer. 'My son has died,' he said, 'the one you said was going to be a lawyer and an official and a governor.' 'By his blessed memory,' the astrologer replied, 'if he had lived, he would have been all of those things.'

Someone else I know was foolish enough to believe a magician's claims that he could take him down to Hades. He instructed him to meet during a full moon, and then on twenty-nine successive mornings took him down to the river Nile to bathe him (they were in Egypt) while reciting a long chant to the rising sun, which seemed to be invoking the spirits of the dead. On the thirtieth day – needless to say, this all cost a lot of money – he spat upon my friend's face and told him to go home without catching the eye of anyone. Each day, they breakfasted on nuts and acorns and drank water specially brought in from Persia, and each night they slept outside on the grass.

Once the magician had decided my friend was sufficiently prepared, he took him at midnight to the river, purified him and rubbed him with oil, all the while muttering a spell, then he made a magic circle around him to protect him from ghosts and finally led him home backwards. He himself put on a magic robe and gave my friend a lion-skin hat to wear and a lyre to carry. He instructed him to bring a large sum of money with which to pay the ferryman. As dawn approached, they returned to the riverbank where they went to a small boat the magician had prepared, complete with sacrificial victims. They floated downstream for some time before entering a marshy lake. Coming to a desolate, shaded spot, they landed and the magician began to dig a hole. They slew lambs and sprinkled their blood around its edge. Meanwhile the magician shouted out an invocation to the dead at the top of his voice. It was completely unintelligible. As he ended, there was a great commotion and my friend thought he heard the barking of Cerberus in the distance but then passed out. When he came to, his head was sore, his money gone and the magician nowhere to be seen. I shall let you draw your own conclusions.

The gods themselves can decide whether to punish such charlatans. We Romans can afford to take a relaxed view towards other religions since, through our scrupulous devotion to the state gods, we ensure that they remain on our side. We incorporate those gods whom we conquer and so expand our divine support alongside

our territory. But we also export our gods to our subjects so that they too may access this overwhelming divine power. Our emperors are deified by vote of the senate on their death and their images are worshipped throughout the empire. Every provincial then understands that it is no disgrace to have been conquered by gods. They can pray and sacrifice for the emperors, their ministers, for the preservation of society and for peace at the same time as they continue to venerate their local deities.

But our tolerance has limits. The health of the state requires the gods to be kept happy. We must be wary of individuals who might offend the gods. For the gods give clear signs, in the form of portents, if they are angry. It is vital, therefore, to keep track of these so that we are able to monitor the divine mood. For that reason, the pontiffs draw up an annual list of whatever significant portents have occurred during the year and post it publicly. Consider, for example, what happened during the reign of that tyrannical emperor, Domitian. Ominous birds landed on the capitol, houses were overturned by an earthquake, and in the ensuing panic the weak were trampled underfoot. A shortage of corn led to famine, all of which was construed as a supernatural warning. And earlier, during the republic, prior to the onset of plague there had been ample evidence of divine ill will: in the territory of Veii a boy had been born with two heads, and elsewhere a girl had been born with teeth. In Campania, there was even ample evidence that a cow had spoken.

Above all, we must be alert to groups who might introduce strange religious practices and thereby unsettle our special relationship with the gods. The Jews are one such sect. The emperor Augustus showed them great tolerance. He knew that many of them lived on the other side of the Tiber and, although they had first come to Rome as slaves, were now Roman citizens because they had been freed by their masters. They had not, however, been forced to change any of their traditions or religious customs, and had set up their own synagogues and kept their own Sabbath day. Augustus also knew that they sent large sums of money back to Jerusalem. But he never tried to drive them out of Rome or deprive them of their rights as Roman citizens. This was because he respected Judaea and its ancient customs and so he behaved with total piety towards the Jews and their religion and even donated money for Jewish rites to be held on his behalf. He made sure they received their fair share of the free corn distribution, particularly if it was given out on a Sabbath day when they would have been unable to collect it. How did they repay this generosity? They rebelled during the time of Nero until the great Vespasian and the divine Titus suppressed the revolt.

A similarly subversive group are the Christians. This group even refuse to sacrifice to the deified emperors for the health of the empire. After the Great Fire of Rome, the emperor Nero naturally blamed this sect who are known to look forward to a time when the world will be destroyed in a great conflagration. He had them thrown to the beasts or covered with pitch and burned to provide street lighting. Even though the Christians were widely hated for their vices and thought deserving of the harshest punishment, people took pity on them because they believed that Nero posed an even greater danger to Rome.

Beware Christianity! To worship their god is to renounce the gods that have made Rome great. It is to see this god as your father and your fellow Christians as brothers and sisters instead of your actual siblings and family. Your real father should be the object of your reverence and respect and you should obey him. It is only natural, then, that from time to time, when the state is in difficulty, it becomes clear that subversive groups such as this are offending the gods and so require suppression. Some of these Christians actively want to be executed. When asked simply to make an offering towards the emperor's statue and taste of the sacrificial meat, they refuse, believing that their one god would be offended by such an act. Why is not clear to me.

I saw some Christians being tried in the forum recently. A huge crowd had come to watch. One by one the accused confessed to being Christians. One girl's father tried to persuade her to offer sacrifice and held up her young baby before her to try to convince her to change her mind. Even the judge joined in, since he had no desire to punish this well-born young lady, saying, 'Take pity on your father. Have mercy on your child.' Her steadfast response was, 'I am a Christian.' It was shameful to see the way she disobeyed her grey-haired father, who was reduced to begging on his knees and even had to be driven back with rods at one point when he rushed at her with his eyes popping out in anger.

The judge had no alternative but to condemn them

all to be thrown to the beasts in the arena. They were to be executed at the games being held to celebrate the emperor's birthday a few days later. The night before the games, the condemned were given their last supper. As was usual, all the local people came to watch and mocked them for their stupidity at not sacrificing to the gods and their hostility towards the emperor by refusing to sacrifice to him. The Christians hurled back their own threats about what their supposedly all-powerful god would do to the Romans, but he hardly seemed to be of much help to them so far.

The next day saw the Christians taken to the arena. Remarkably, most of them seemed to be smiling. When the young mother was led out into the arena, she was stripped naked. Since she had recently given birth her breasts were still dripping with milk. The crowd were understandably shocked at this indecent sight and demanded that she be taken out of the arena and clothed properly before being brought in to face her death. The crowd bayed for the Christians' blood. They responded by singing, which was no fun at all. Some of the men shouted out slogans like 'You judge us but God will judge you!', which just infuriated the crowd still more. The governor had the criminals whipped. The Christians shouted out thanks to their god for their suffering – they are a strange bunch.

A wild boar, a bear and a leopard were unleashed on the men, who had been tied to a raised platform in the middle of the arena where all the spectators could get a good view. They prayed out loud but their god did not hear them. There was a very funny moment when the leopard grabbed one of the men by the face and so much blood spurted out that everyone shouted out, 'Enjoy your shower!' After their bodies were dragged off, a particularly savage wild cow was set on the women. You could tell that the young mother was from a good family because when her clothing was ripped she modestly tried to pull the tear together in order to cover her naked thigh. She even searched for a pin to tie up her dishevelled hair. Battered to a pulp by this beast, the young mother was eventually put out of her misery by a gladiator. He was a novice and his hand shook so much that he missed with his first blow and merely wounded her. The woman showed an admirable nerve and actually had to guide the sword to her own neck before he was able to kill her with a downward thrust.

The story of the young woman reminds me of the fable about the man who was shipwrecked and, as he trod water, kept calling on Athena for help while the other sailors swam away. Eventually one of the others shouted out, 'Kick your legs to help Athena.' As the fable correctly points out, we cannot expect the gods to do everything. We think and act to help our own cause. All that the silly girl had to do was to make a simple offering and she would have been free. Instead, she is dead, her family desolate and her poor child is motherless.

We all have some divine spirit within us, who makes a note of our good and bad actions and keeps a protective eye on us. No man could be good without that inner force and we must do all we can to develop it. We worship any place where a divine presence is evident: ancient groves of gnarled trees that shut out the sun's rays;

deep caves on a mountainside that have been hollowed out by nature's strength; hot springs; or the sources of mighty rivers. All these we adore as being redolent with the divine. Well, the same is true of some people. If you ever see someone who is calm in the midst of danger, who can resist desire and temptation, who is happy in adversity, who seems elevated above others and almost godlike in his serenity, then you can recognise a similar divine presence as we find in nature. This is what you too must aim to achieve. Through prayer and devotion, you can develop your inner soul and thereby leave behind the cares and fears of earth. When a soul has risen above mere mortals, is completely in control of its own emotions, and passes through whatever events fickle fortune throws its way with unshakeable equanimity, then it has acquired something of the force of heaven.

·· COMMENTARY ··

Traditional Roman religion involved endless, accurate repetition for its effect. Examples of the details can be found in Pliny the Elder's *Natural History* (28.10–11) and Cato the Elder's *On Agriculture* (134, 139–41). Augustine mocked the sheer number of Roman gods that existed for even the minor parts of an ear of corn in his *City of God* (4.8). There were many different festivals, often associated with traditional rural practice at different points in the year. The Robigalia are described in Ovid *Fasti* (4.905–41)

and the Lupercalia in Plutarch's *Life of Romulus* 21.Vestal Virgins and the dreadful punishments awaiting those of them who erred are detailed by Aulus Gellius in his *Attic Nights* (1.12) and Dionysius of Halicarnassus (2.67).

The divine was thought to be everywhere, so it made perfect sense to look for the will of the gods to be revealed in all manner of natural phenomena, from birds to dreams. The flexible attitude towards the interpretation of such omens can be found in Livy's *History of Rome* 10.40 and Suetonius *Tiberius* 2.The account of visiting an oracular cave is from Maximus of Tyre *Discourses* 26, while the story of the charlatan necromancer can be read in Lucian's *Menippus*. The list of things people looked to these popular religious practices for help with is based on the headings of the chapters in Dorotheus of Sidon's astrological handbook.

Sacrifice in Roman religion served as the means of communication between the human and the divine. This did not always involve the slaughter of animals, which tended to be kept back for more important ceremonies. Incense – a simple mix of a variety of aromatic plants and oils – was the most common form of offering to the gods. The rituals in which such offerings took place varied considerably. At the larger end of the scale, there were imperial festivals and local processions through a city's streets, but there were many small-scale, private acts of devotion in simple shrines or within the home. The gods were believed to love the sweet smell of incense and this made it an excellent way to approach them for help. But they also relished garlands of flowers and burnt offerings, all of which curled upwards to them in the heavens. The early Christians had often refused to take part in sacrifice, even if it only entailed the burning of incense. Pliny the Younger, as governor of Bithynia in the early second century AD, went so far as to execute several Christians on the grounds that they refused to offer incense to the Roman gods and thereby risked offending them (see his *Letters* 10.96). Unsurprisingly, many Christians gave in to the threats and torture that were sometimes applied to them and did offer sacrifice. These traitors were dismissively known by other Christians as 'incense-burners'. It is a sign of how much the Christian Church later came to an accommodation with traditional pagan practice that incense came to play such a central role in the rituals of Catholicism and the pope came to be known as the Pontifex Maximus.

Romans believed that the gods were on their side. They referred to this rather cosy arrangement as the *Pax Deorum* – the peace of the gods. It seemed perfectly reasonable to ascribe positive outcomes in human affairs to divine will. Similarly, misfortune was understood as a scourge sent by the gods to punish Rome for any social or political acts that had upset their divine sensibilities. Persecuting those who threatened to bring divine wrath down on Rome was a natural corollary of these attitudes. The description of the martyrdom is based on the account of St Perpetua's death in AD 203 in Carthage, one of the rare ancient texts to have been authored by a woman. The fate of the Christians after the Great Fire under Nero is in Tacitus *Annals* 15.44. But we should not see these dramatic persecutions as the norm. Rome's pagan religion was, in reality, a broad set of religious practices, which lacked the centralised orthodoxy of later Christianity, so there was no intrinsic drive to stamp out religious difference or innovation. It was usually only when the community felt actively threatened that persecution followed. The numbers involved were generally fairly small, as the state lacked the capacity to persecute in a systematic way. We can see it as a simple form of scapegoating that was designed to be a powerful symbolic reaffirmation of traditional morality, rather than as measures that aimed to eradicate alternative religious groups. Nor was it only Christians who were persecuted. Magicians, astrologers and Dionysus worshippers all suffered at the hands of the Roman state at certain times. Judaism was granted the status of a permitted religion by Julius Caesar and then Augustus on account of its great antiquity (see, for example, Philo *Embassy to Gaius* 155–8).

Importing the cult of the Great Mother, or Cybele, as she was also known, was the flip side of the same belief system. If the current gods weren't working then try looking to a new one. It is possible that the Romans had failed to realise quite what worship of this cult involved, with its self-castration and flamboyant effeminacy. But the diplomats who negotiated the transfer must have had some idea and perhaps the whole point was that the situation was so difficult, with Hannibal on the doorstep, that something radically different had to be tried. In any case, the Aeneas myth gave a neat way to link the new goddess with Rome's ancient ancestors. The story of the introduction of the Sibylline books can be found in Dionysius of Halicarnassus (4.62). Macrobius's *Saturnalia*

(3.9.7–8) has the formula that was said to win over an enemy's gods to Rome's side.

Rome's huge conquests and open attitude towards divine immigration meant that over time they accumulated a wide variety of new religious practices. During the first three centuries of the empire, there was a steady move in favour of these new religions, many of which took their inspiration from the East, such as Mithraism, Christianity, Isis worship and Manichaeism. Romans seemed to be looking for a more personal and intimate relationship with the divine than traditional pagan rituals could offer. These new religions also offered a greater degree of spiritual progress, with the believer moving closer to the divine by means of devotion, belief and ethical behaviour, and this is reflected in Falx's final section, which is based on the Stoicism of Seneca *Letters* 41. Constantine's conversion to Christianity in AD 312 needs to be understood within this larger context. Christian sources would have us believe that it was both heartfelt and inevitable, but the larger religious trend was already well established in Roman society. Christianity also happened to suit Constantine's political ambitions to reunify the empire after it had split between rival claimants to the throne. Like his predecessor, Diocletian, Constantine also wanted a far more powerful and centralised state. Once he had succeeded in becoming sole emperor, he wanted a religion to reflect the new, more powerful unity. Now there would be one God, one empire, one emperor.

CHAPTER IX

LIVE FOREVER!

GLORY. IF YOU HAVE LEARNED one thing in this book, it should be the importance of glory to the true Roman. However lowly your position in society, you still have it within you to carry out the noblest deeds. Your final act should also be your finest. What better way to cement your position in the annals of eternal fame than by dying beautifully. Ask the gods for one thing: a stout heart that has no fear of death. For if you die bravely, you will win a glory that is more lasting than bronze. Your name will live forever.

In truth, who wants to live to see bitter old age? After the age of forty, you see nothing new in life. You have experienced all it has to offer and have little time to achieve much else. A long life merely brings acquaintance with a thousand misfortunes. There are some benefits, of course: wisdom, moderation, calm, a softening of the ferocity of youth, to say nothing of some peace and quiet. But there are many more drawbacks – creaking bones, a weakening of the mind, the death of family and friends. There is nothing worse than to bury your own children. Laugh in the face of death. The day after my own son died I met his teacher in the street. 'I'm sorry Marcus wasn't at school yesterday,' I said, 'but he's dead.'

Make sure you plan a proper funeral. When I die, I have left instructions that, as when any illustrious man passes away, my body is to be carried to the rostra in the forum, held up in a conspicuous upright posture for all to see. My surviving son, or, if he too has died by that point, my brother, will then deliver a speech outlining my virtues and achievements. As the assembled crowd are reminded of all the things I did – the shows I held on their behalf, the banquets I put on at my expense – they will be moved to such regret at my passing that they will join the throng of mourners. After the cremation and the interment of the ashes in the Falx family tomb, an image of me will be placed in the hallway of my villa, enclosed in a wooden shrine. This image is a life-like mask of me that I have already had made, so I could approve of its accuracy. In later years, my family will decorate this image along with those of my ancestors whenever there is a public festival. And they will bring my image along to family funerals and have it worn by a man who closely resembles me in stature and gait. This man will wear a toga with a purple border since I am of senatorial rank. What more impressive sight can there be than to see our illustrious predecessors paraded before us as if still alive? What spectacle could be more glorious than this? The speaker of the oration recounts the great deeds, not only of the dead man, but also those of all the other deceased whose images are present. In this way, the fame of those who won glory in the service of Rome is made immortal. Most important of all, the young men watching are inspired to endure anything for the public good so that they too might win the eternal glory that awaits the brave.

Your will should reward those who have done you good service in life. I shall, for example, free all my personal slaves who have served me well. Do not be so vulgar as to go on about your generosity while you are still alive. But it is beneficial for your slaves to know if they are to be freed on your death as it ensures they will behave well before then. If you do not possess a family tomb, make sure you build a monument appropriate to your station in life. Less is more in this regard. I saw one freedman's tomb recently that was ornately carved with wreaths, jars of perfume, small dogs and various mythological scenes. It must have been a hundred feet wide and two hundred deep. It was surrounded by fruit trees and vines. A slave was permanently stationed at its entrance to stop people defecating there. The statue of the deceased showed him in the garb of an office he could never possibly have held and had him wearing various pieces of jewellery. He was shown handing out money to the people. Then beside him stood statues of his wife and favourite slave boy. A sundial had been placed in the middle of the tomb's front so that anyone wanting to know the time would also have to look at his name carved in colossal letters above it. Beneath it, an inscription bragged about how rich he was and finished with an exhortation to 'Never listen to Philosophers', which may well be sensible advice but hardly needs shouting about.

If you are not wealthy, you might consider the following selection from modest inscriptions I have seen: 'Here is my home forever; here is a rest from toil'; 'Into nothing from nothing how quickly we go'; 'The god of wine never let me down'; and the ever popular, 'I was not, I was, I am not, I don't care'. Build your monument by the side of one of the roads out of town so that passers-by and travellers will see you. I know a good joke about this. Some people once recommended a particular spot to an egghead who was asking about the best place in which to build his tomb. 'That's no good,' he complained, 'it's in a very unhealthy area.'

Die well. There is no point living a virtuous and brave life if you squeal like a pig when death approaches. Dying properly is one of life's duties. You could have no better example than Seneca. He had once been the childhood tutor to the future emperor Nero, and had for a while acted as his adviser when he ascended to the throne. But Seneca had soon fallen foul of the emperor (possibly because of his involvement in a plot to have him assassinated, although some claim he was innocent). Ordered to commit suicide, Seneca chose the traditional method. He dictated his last words to a scribe, then, surrounded by his closest friends, he cut the veins of his wrists and those behind the knees. All the while, he conversed with his companions and maintained a dignified self-composure comparable to that of Socrates when he drank hemlock at his execution. His advanced age and poor diet meant that the blood did not flow freely. He drank a dose of poison to accelerate his lingering death but this had no effect. He therefore ordered his slaves to carry him into a hot bath to make his veins bleed more profusely. Even this proved ineffectual and the soldiers who had been sent to witness the suicide started to threaten that they would finish the job themselves. So Seneca was removed to an extremely hot bath and was quickly suffocated by the steam. As he had directed in his will, he was buried without any of the usual funeral rites. Such was his virtue that even when at the height of his power he had been thinking about ending his life modestly.

Women too can die gloriously. When Caecina Paetus was ordered to kill himself after being charged with disloyalty to the emperor Claudius, he revealed his cowardice by losing his nerve when the time came to plunge the sword into his guts. His wife, Arria, took the sword and stabbed herself, then handed it to him, saying, 'See, Paetus, it doesn't hurt.'

Even foreign women can enjoy a noble death. The last of the Ptolemies in Egypt, Cleopatra, foiled the plans of the emperor Augustus to display her alive in his triumph at Rome to celebrate his defeat of the queen and her lover, Mark Antony. She preferred to leave the world still a queen rather than appear before the Roman people as a captive. She therefore summoned her two most trustworthy attendants, called Naeira and Carmione, and had one arrange her hair beautifully while the other trimmed her nails. They then smuggled in an asp past the guards, concealed in a basket of grapes and figs. It was the type of asp called a 'spitter', which bites with perfect aim and whose venom is deadly. Her two attendants volunteered to test the snake on themselves to make sure that the poison killed, which it swiftly did. Cleopatra then turned the snake on herself. Augustus was amazed, both by the devotion the two women showed towards their queen, but also by Cleopatra's determination not to live like a slave. They say that she died holding her crown on her head so she might look like a queen even in death.

We have seen that a gladiator can redeem himself in death. When the winner takes his sword and places it on the neck of the defeated gladiator, the loser must look ahead with a firm gaze, showing no sign of fear or emotion. Condemned criminals can also reveal remarkable bravery through how they choose to die. Recently I heard of a German captive who had been sentenced to fight wild beasts in the arena – an agonising death. The morning of the show, he went to the latrine to relieve himself – this being the only act he could do unattended by a guard – then he grabbed the sponge stick used to clean one's backside and shoved it down his throat, choking himself to death. Not very elegant but what bravery! And in another example, a gladiator was being carried along to the arena in a cart. Nodding his head as if he were falling asleep, he suddenly pushed his head between the spokes of the wheel and broke his neck. He escaped his wretched fate by means of the very wagon that was carrying him to his punishment.

We must never be surprised at the tragedies fate sends our way. It is the lot of humans to suffer a variety of calamities and misfortunes. Many people fear death. But all death is the same. Some people even abandoned Campania after Vesuvius erupted there and said they would never visit the region again. They are deluded if they think any part of the world is exempt from danger.

All areas live under the same divine laws. Fate travels in a circle and eventually always comes back to places it has not visited for a long time.

The wise do not fear fate. If you have wisdom you know that possessions and power, even your own body, belong to you only temporarily. But the wise also know that their lives are not worthless, for the very reason that their lives do not belong to them. Whatever they have, they have on trust, to be returned to the gods whenever they so command. They perform all their duties as carefully as a pious and scrupulous man would take care of property left in his charge as a trustee. When he has to hand it back, he does not complain or rail against fortune, but simply says, 'I thank you for what I have had possession of and while it was in my care I managed to increase it, but now I give it back to you willingly.' So when nature summons back your life, you should say also to her, 'Take back my spirit, which is better than when you gave it me.' What hardship can there be in returning to the place where you came from?

You cannot live well unless you know how to die well. We hate gladiators if they are desperate to save their lives by any cowardly trick, but we love them if they are brave to the point of recklessness. So too the gods are more likely to torment us and kill us if we cling to our lives. Our lives are the gods' gladiatorial games. 'Why should I spare you,' they say, 'you cowardly creature? You will be hacked at and wounded all the more because you do not know how to offer your throat to the sword.' But to the brave, the gods say, 'You, who receive the blow without drawing away your neck or putting up your hands to stop it, shall both live longer and die more quickly and painlessly.'

Misfortune only hurts those who have not expected it and so are unprepared to meet it. Those whose attention has been directed only towards happiness find the pain of tragedy impossible to bear. We see disasters all around us in the world. Why should we be surprised when one finally affects us? It is too late to train the spirit once disaster has struck. Understand that life is transitory and that however rich or powerful or healthy you now are, this will soon pass. Was not Julius Caesar assassinated just at the acme of his power? Was not King Jugurtha, who struck fear into the Romans, defeated within the same year? How many other kings and queens have we seen paraded before us as captives in Rome? In a world of change, you must expect that whatever can happen to you, will happen to you. This will give you the strength to cope with it when it does.

We cannot know how many years the gods will permit us on this earth. Even as you read this, your life is slipping away. So grab the present and act now to improve your life. This spirit of self-help, guided by the will of the gods, is the root of all genuine success. No individual can succeed on his own, but too much help from others weakens the spirit, for whatever is done for a man takes away his need to do it for himself. Whenever you are helped too much the result is that it makes you helpless. Your character is moulded by a thousand subtle influences: by family, by life's experiences, by books, by friends, by neighbours and enemies. But however great their influence undoubtedly is, it is still abundantly clear that you must be the active agent of your own happiness and success.

If you follow the guidance of this book, you too will be able to attain the best that Rome has to offer: to become a gentleman of leisure, with a large income drawn from substantial estates. You will own a considerable household full of obedient children and slaves. You will know how to develop habits of health, good manners and ease, without ever wallowing in luxury. With a stout and courageous heart, you will have the gods on your side. An inspiration to those you lead, you will be honest, honourable and unwavering in your constancy. Above all, you will be willing to sacrifice everything for the good of Rome.

·· COMMENTARY ··

Falx's final section of advice is drawn from various philosophical writings. It reflects primarily the Stoicism of Seneca, whose death Falx describes (based on Tacitus's account in *Annals* 15; for Seneca's Stoic texts, see, for example, *Letters* 70 and his *On the Calm Mind*). Such thought was popular among the upper classes in Rome during the empire, most famously with the emperor Marcus Aurelius, who wrote a collection of *Meditations* along similar lines. This pragmatic philosophy may reflect something of the tough Roman spirit traditionally associated with all Romans, but it was also a Greek import. Founded by the philosopher Zeno, Stoicism was very much a way of life – living in accordance with nature – with an emphasis on how one behaved rather than what one said or argued. The popularity of Stoicism, with its passive, resigned acceptance of what fate sends your way, may also have reflected the loss of power by Rome's political class once the emperors were in control. What else could you do in the face of Nero's whims?

Dio Cassius's *History of Rome* (60.16) has the story of Arria, the brave wife of Caecina Paetus. The description of the upper-class funeral comes from Polybius *Histories* 6.53. The jokes are to be found in the one surviving ancient joke book, *The Laughter-Lover*. The black humour on display was perhaps one way in which Romans coped with the high levels of mortality and the fact that death could come suddenly. Petronius's *Satyricon* offers the gauche tomb of the nouveau riche character Trimalchio, who is desperate to impress even in death. The lesser tombstone inscriptions can be found in the *Carmina Latina Epigraphica* (for example, numbers 143, 225, 856 and 1495).

Falx's stress on glory and a good death reminds us of Horace's lines *Dulce et decorum est pro patria mori* – 'It is sweet and glorious to die for your country' (*Odes* 3.2). The First World War did much to end such outright enthusiasm for heroism. Falx's emphasis on the need for the individual to act within a communal context is also at odds with much of the modern focus on personal freedoms and self-development. But there is much we can still learn from his strength in the face of adversity. And in a world where, according to the United Nations, more than a billion people live on less than a dollar a day, and 2.7 billion on under two dollars, we should perhaps be mindful that western individualism is a luxury most can still ill afford.

FURTHER READING

THE MODERN SELF-HELP BOOK was invented by the aptly named Samuel Smiles, whose *Self-help: With Illustrations of Character and Conduct* became a Victorian bestseller. The phenomenon can partly be explained by the fact that traditional folk wisdom no longer seemed adequate for a society undergoing the rapid changes brought about by industrialisation. People also found themselves more distanced from sources of such traditional advice because of leaving the countryside to live in cities. In addition, the growing emphasis on the individual instead of the community placed greater pressure on individuals to 'find themselves' and to invent their own personality. Since then, the self-help industry has boomed. Dale Carnegie's *How to Win Friends and Influence People* (1936) sold 15 million copies, while Napoleon Hill's *Think and Grow Rich* (1937) notched up an extraordinary 70 million sales. Other notable contributions to the genre include *The Power of Positive Thinking* (1952), *The Seven Habits of Highly Effective People* (1989), *Who Moved my Cheese* (1998) and *The Secret* (2006). Books more focused on mental and sexual health include *You Can Heal Your Life* (1984) and *Men are from Mars, Women*

are from Venus (1992). The self-help genre was neatly satirised by Stephen Potter in the 1940s and 1950s in his books *Gamesmanship* and *One-Upmanship* and, more recently, by the *Bridget Jones's Diary* series.

Self-help may be a modern invention but it is not without antecedents in the ancient world. Often published under the banner of philosophy, many ancient texts sought to improve the all-round well-being of individuals by helping them to live better lives and to cope with the inevitable misfortunes that would come their way. These books were primarily written by and for the wealthier members of society, who could afford to indulge in such contemplative practices. The commentaries have already provided details of some of the more important texts, above all those of Cicero and Seneca, while Ovid offered much advice about how to improve one's love life. More popular practical wisdom can be found in such things as proverbs and fables, and these are analysed by Teresa Morgan in her book *Popular Morality in the Early Roman Empire* (Cambridge University Press, 2007).

Good translations of the primary texts can be found in the Loeb Classical Library or in the various sourcebooks listed below. General sourcebooks include:

Lewis, N. and Reinhold, M. (eds), *Roman Civilization: A Sourcebook* (Harper & Row, 1966).

Parkin, T. G. and Pomeroy, A. J., *Roman Social History: A Sourcebook* (Routledge, 2007).

Shelton, J., *As the Romans Did: A Sourcebook in*

Roman Social History (Oxford University Press, 1998).

The best recent introductions to Roman history are Mary Beard's *SPQR* (Profile, 2015) and Christopher Kelly's *The Roman Empire: A Very Short Introduction* (Oxford University Press, 2006). Readers may also find useful my own *The Ancient World* (Profile, 2015).

Those interested in looking at Roman emotional life should consult Kaster, R.A., *Emotion, Restraint, and Community in Ancient Rome* (Oxford University Press, 2005), while the role played by women in Roman domestic emotional life is explored in Richlin, A., 'Emotional Work: Lamenting the Roman Dead', in E. Tylawsky and C. Weiss (eds), *Essays in Honor of Gordon Williams: Twenty-five Years at Yale* (H. R. Schwab, 2001), pp. 229–48. The centrality of work to Roman identity is examined in Sandra Joshel's book, *Work, Identity, and Legal Status at Rome: A Study of the Occupational Inscriptions* (University of Oklahoma Press, 1992).

Ancient sexuality was constructed in a way that was profoundly different from modern western notions. Many interesting primary sources can be found in Johnson, M. and Ryan, T., *Sexuality in Greek and Roman Society and Literature: A Sourcebook* (Routledge, 2005), while homosexual texts can be accessed in Hubbard, T. K., *Homosexuality in Greece and Rome: A Sourcebook of Basic Documents* (University of California Press, 2003). These are discussed at length in Williams, C. A., *Roman Homosexuality: Ideologies of Masculinity in Classical Antiquity* (Oxford University Press, 1999). Household documentary evidence is gathered together in Gardener, J., *The Roman Household: A Sourcebook* (Routledge, 1991), and in Judith Evans Grubbs's work, *Women and the law in the Roman Empire: A Sourcebook on Marriage, Divorce and Widowhood* (Routledge, 2002).

The best place to start for those readers looking to dig deeper into the phenomenon of the Roman games is the excellent sourcebook of translated primary material by Alison Futrell, *The Roman Games: A Sourcebook* (Blackwell, 2006). This offers a wide variety of interesting texts with informed and illuminating commentary. I have written an introductory guide to the games: *The Day Commodus Killed a Rhino: Understanding the Roman Games* (Johns Hopkins University Press, 2014). Mary Beard's book, *Pompeii: The Life of a Roman Town* (Profile, 2008), has a useful chapter on the spectacles: 'Fun and Games'. Those interested in the lives of ordinary Romans can look at my *Popular Culture in Ancient Rome* (Polity, 2009) and will find many useful sources collected in Cooley, A. E. and Cooley, M. G. L., *Pompeii and Herculaneum: A Sourcebook* (Routledge, 2014). My *Leisure in Ancient Rome* (Polity, 1995) looks at the cultural importance of leisure to Roman society as a whole.

Ancient medicine covers a huge array of writers and texts. The Roman medic Galen was a prolific writer whose nineteenth-century edition runs to more than twenty thousand pages. A translated selection can be found in Singer, P. N., *Galen: Selected Works* (Oxford University Press, 1997). Excellent introductions to ancient medicine have been written by Helen King, *Greek and Roman Medicine* (Bloomsbury, 2013) and Vivian Nutton,

Ancient Medicine (Routledge, 2005). The second chapter of my book, *Popular Culture in Ancient Rome* (Polity, 2009), looks at mental health in the Roman world.

The close relationship between medicine and religion is explored in Ogden, D., *Magic, Witchcraft, and Ghosts in the Greek and Roman Worlds: A Sourcebook* (Oxford University Press, 2002) and Barton, T. S., *Power and Knowledge: Astrology, Physiognomics, and Medicine under the Roman Empire* (University of Michigan Press, 1994). Roman religion is examined in Beard, M., North, J. and Price, S., *Religions of Rome* (Cambridge University Press, 1998), and in Rüpke, J., *Religion of the Romans* (Polity, 2007). Translated magical texts from Roman Egypt can be found in Betz, H. D. (ed.), *The Greek Magical Papyri in Translation, Including the Demotic Spells* (University of Chicago Press, 1992), while many other magical texts are discussed in Gager, J. G. (ed.), *Curse Tablets and Binding Spells from the Ancient World* (Oxford University Press, 1992). Ancient attitudes towards suicide are examined in van Hooff, A. J. L., *From Autothanasia to Suicide: Self-Killing in Classical Antiquity* (Routledge, 1990).

INDEX